REDEEMING

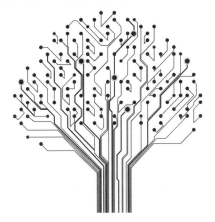

MEMORY

REDEEMING

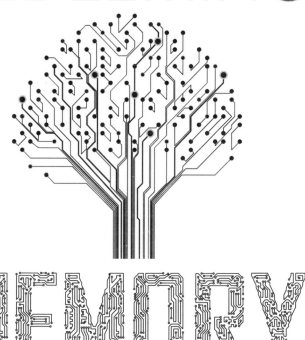

MEMORY

How God Transforms Memories
from a Heavy Burden to a Blessed Hope

MATT REHRER, M.D.

In the midst of despair, the psalmists remembered God's steadfast love. At the cross, God remembers our sins no more. Such references to memory interweave throughout Scripture, and remind us that walking with Christ begins with remembering what he has done. In Redeeming Memory, Dr. Rehrer invites you to journey with him on an exploration of memory: its biological scaffolding, its role in the Bible, and its significance in Christian discipleship. Drawing from the wisdom of the Puritans, his knowledge of biology, and a keen understanding of Scripture, Dr. Rehrer points us to the God who remains faithful, even when we forget him. Read this book slowly, and remember that the Lord is good.

KATHRYN BUTLER, MD: Author of *Between Life and Death, Glimmers of Grace,* and *The Dream Keeper Saga*

Weaving his experiences in the ER, remembrances of his late family, and illustrations from the natural world, Dr. Matthew Rehrer walks the reader from the Garden of Eden to final Glory, examining the purpose, process, and redemption of memory. Dr. Rehrer's medical, historical, and theologically devotional musings will not soon be forgotten.

DR. LISA LaGEORGE: Director of CHF Academy at Children's Hunger Fund

I am always interested in books by authors who have a deeply personal reason for writing them. Redeeming memories is just that kind of book. Out of the crucible of great personal loss, Matthew Rehrer has given us a great gift. This book is a thorough look at what the Bible says about our memories. Most of us have experiences that we wish we could forget. This book tells us from Scripture how God intends to use those memories for our good and His glory. I recommend this book to those who want to know what the Bible says about God's great gift of our memories.

CHARLES D. HODGES JR, MD: Executive Director Vision of Hope; Family Physician

Remembering is a compelling theme in all of Scripture. It drives worship, obedience, and a Christ-centered life. It reflects God's own nature. Do it wrong, and one ends up in delusion and distraction. Do it right, and one ends up in a life that honors Christ. I am most thankful for Rehrer's work on this most important topic as it comprehensively covers this vital truth both theologically and practically. It is a deep and insightful dive into what will change your life.

ABNER CHOU, Ph.D.: Interim President and John F. MacArthur Endowed Fellow, The Master's University

It is a joy to see relevant, gospel-centered, biblical material being written on topics that impact us every day. I am pleased to commend Dr. Matt Rehrer's work on memory, which is the first of its kind that I can recall to mind. Dr. Rehrer's background and insight into this topic is easy enough to read for the average reader, while still being well-researched and detailed. I was eager to learn about memory—both its purposes and how God will ultimately redeem it—in this small tome. I'm confident readers will be edified and encouraged to learn of how we all can use our memory to better glorify the Lord.

JONATHAN D. HOLMES: Executive Director, Fieldstone Counseling; Pastor of Counseling, Parkside Church Green

Redeeming Memory
How God Transforms Memories
from a Heavy Burden to a Blessed Hope
Matt Rehrer, M.D.

Copyright © 2022 Shepherd Press

ISBNS:
Paper: 978-1-63342-267-4
epub: 978-1-63342-268-1
mobi: 978-1-63342-269-8

Cover design and typeset by www.greatwriting.org

Printed in the United States of America

Shepherd Press
P.O. Box 24
Wapwallopen, PA 18660
www.shepherdpress.com

Table of Contents

Introduction 13

The Foundation of Memory 17

The Malady of Memory 35

The Cudgel of Corrupted Memory 55

God's Remedy for Memory 65

Tools to Sanctify Memory 81

Cues to Sanctify Memory 95

The Keys of Redemptive Memory 117

The Fruit of Redemptive Memory 141

Man's Corruption of Future Remembrance 161

God's Redemption of Future Remembrance 181

God's Forever Remembrance 205

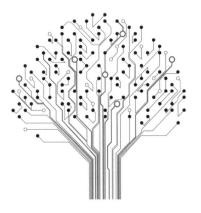

Dedication

In memory of my dad Bill, mom Pam, sisters Bethany and Amy, and father-in-law Lonnie who all rest with the God who never forgets.

This I recall to mind,
Therefore I have hope.
The Lord's lovingkindnesses
Indeed never cease,
For His compassions never fail.
They are new every morning;
Great is Your faithfulness.
Lamentations 3:21–23

Acknowledgments

This book was not written on the sands of an island but in the center of community. It flows out of the collective contributions of many.

I first would like to thank my church family and staff. You shaped this book through conversations but also your faithful living. I am grateful to my friends, Jeremy Pray and Matt Fitch, who inspired the first thoughts on biblical memory on a long car ride to a conference. My friend and pastor, Kent Dresdow, you encouraged me to write and influenced these pages through your preaching and counsel. Jonathan Holmes, my friend, thank you. You moved this book from a wishful thought to a published reality through your kind advice and helpful introductions. Jim Holmes and Shepherd Press, thank you for taking a risk on an unknown and unpublished author. It has been a blessing to work with you. Amy Wenslawski and Rachel Haislet, your editing provided clarity and removed distractions.

My wife and best friend, Kara, you stood by me, listened to me, and supported me from start to finish. The etchings of this book come from a pen that we held together. To my kids, Haddon, Elsie, and Myles, I love you. Don't forget to "Remember your Creator in the days of your youth (Eccl. 12:1)."

To my Lord and Savior, You remember me even when I forget You. Even when the words of this book fade away, Your Word will stand forever.

Introduction

Formaldehyde wafted through the air. A white-haired man with a lab coat and large-framed glasses instructed us to unlatch our metal tanks. As the doors swung open, we made the rite of passage into medicine and met death. As a first-year medical student, I began to encounter the ironies of medicine. The foundation of medical practice, which works to preserve life, started with an examination of preserved death. A mistake here in the anatomy lab on the dead would be exceedingly safer than a mistake on the living.

The anatomy textbook sat on a stand at the end of my station propped open to the first page. The scalpel unzipped the body and unzipped the emotions of excitement mingled with questions. In a preservation of humanness, our group left the face covered as we worked. The initial awe of anatomy was soon replaced by the academics of anatomy. Page one now turned into page one hundred. The lessons focused on identification of structures: nerves, blood vessels, ligaments, muscles, and bones.

The day finally arrived to study the brain, the mysterious three-pound organ that housed the memories. The identity of structures jolted into thoughts about the identity of the cadaveric person. The face remained covered, but questions inundated my mind about her. What was she like? What did she believe? Whom did she influence? Does anyone remember her? The use of my memory to retain facts about the human body helped me see something deeper: the significance of memory to a person's identity.

I did not fully grasp the significance of memory in the anatomy lab until death interjected into my personal life. It is one thing to examine the death of an unknown cadaver but quite another to reflect upon the deaths of my dad, mom, and two sisters. Their sudden deaths in a car accident prompted a wrestling with memory and its meaning. This book resulted from my study on memory and what the Bible has to say about it. Memory is important in the Christian life both in its proper function but also in its corruption.

This book is written for Christians who suffer knowingly or unknowingly from the heavy burdens of memory. These burdens, like bitterness or shame, afflict you with seemingly endless reverberations in your thoughts. Do you ever wonder if the vicious cycle will ever end? Will the repeating loops ever be broken? Perhaps you are like me and did not recognize the influence of memory in these unrelenting miseries. This book examines memory through the prism of the gospel to find hope in the midst of misery. Through God's redemptive plan, memory transforms from a *millstone* to a *milestone*. God removes the burdens of memory and enlivens hope in His redemption.

Some may object to using the Bible as the primary source to examine memory. Shouldn't memory be addressed from a scientific viewpoint? Part of my interest in this topic originated from my background in science and medicine as an emergency medicine physician. Throughout the book, the science of memory will be introduced but will coincide with, and not contradict, biblical truth. God designed human memory and knows how best to utilize it for His good purposes.

Biblical memory is a neglected topic in current Christian literature, but God provided gleanings from sermons and books in my research. John Bunyan's *Pilgrim's Progress* gives an illustration of the main character, Christian, and his companion, Hopeful, in their journey that detours to Doubting Castle. Augustine shows that even though he lived in the fourth century, his book *Confessions* applies to the twenty-first century. Puritan preachers like Richard Sibbes (1577–1635), Anthony Burgess (1600–1633), Thomas Watson (1620–1686), Jonathan Edwards (1703–1758), among others, provide a depth and breadth on the mind of God that inspires a desire to think deeply. This book draws from the fearless curiosity of C.S. Lewis as he asks difficult questions. Finally, Charles Haddon Spurgeon (1834–1892) contributes with his insightful observations and analogies. Even still, all of these wise men were guided by, and bend the knee to, the authority of Scripture, the only true infallible source of wisdom.

I seek to build a framework for memory on the familiar structure of the gospel. The book is organized into two sections to address present memory followed by future remembrance.

In the first section, I define memory from a scientific and theological standpoint. God's perfect memory and the creation account establish the original purpose for memory: to glorify and worship God. Next, the fall of Adam and Eve inaugurates the corruption of human memory that bends away from glorifying God to glorifying self. After examining the ways human memory harms, hope springs. God redeems human memory through Christ who was forsaken at the cross and remembered at the resurrection. The next chapters examine God's provisions and promises to help transform memory through the Holy Spirit and end with the hope-filled effects of a redeemed memory.

The second section shifts to future remembrance and its burdens with fears of futility and insignificance; however, God restores future remembrance to Him. The book concludes with the hope of redemptive remembrance and its present effects on earth and future effects in heaven. We will trace memory from the garden of Eden in Genesis to the halls of heaven in Revelation. The big arc of redemption applies to the personal story of each reader with profound implications of hope.

Just like in medicine, a foundation in the classroom prepares for application in the hospital. Human anatomy class, study of the dead, is the first step towards the practice of medicine, care for the living. I hope the study of memory will lead to practical application in God-glorifying daily living.

Introduction
Application Questions

1. In preparation for the first chapter, how would you define memory?

2. How did you respond to a person or event that caused misery in your past? How are you responding to this person or event now?

3. Identify any past spiritual milestones in your life. How do these deepen your faith in the present?

4. Do you battle with a desire to be remembered on earth by others? How has this desire manifested itself in your life?

1

The Foundation of Memory

Time marches forward; memory traces backward. After sixteen years, the front oak trees still stood like two sentries, although they were taller, and the front door was now painted a different color. The house looked ordinary from the outside but was filled with meaning on the inside. As I stood in the driveway, my mind entered through the front door and crossed into the rooms that danced in the past with people, pleasure, and purpose. This home with my memories offered no prospects to create future ones because the occupants who live in my memory no longer lived in the house.

My dad, mom, and two sisters moved from this childhood home in San Antonio to Amarillo in 2004. This same year also marked the start of marriage and first year of medical school in Houston. Despite living in the same state as my parents and two sisters, six hundred miles of flat plains with cattle and oil rigs separated us. On July 8, 2005, my family started the long drive down I-45 to help my new wife and me move into an apartment. Listening to worship music and drinking Sonic slushies, they traveled closer to us. Instantaneously, my family's destination changed from Houston to heaven. My dad, mom, and two sisters went from making memories in the present to being a memory of the past.

On that dreadful night, while still watching and waiting for them, a 911 dispatcher confirmed four deaths that involved a vehicle that matched my sister's car. Trembling, I opened my Bible to Psalm 73. Through tears, I cried "Whom have I in heaven but You? And besides You I desire nothing on the earth. My flesh and my heart may fail, but God is the strength of my heart and my portion forever." God graciously supplied His words as my words to Him. My earthly father now joined my heavenly Father in worship, from singing praise songs in the car to singing praise songs at the throne. The mile marker at the site of the accident marked the finish line of their earthly race.

Whirling, the days that followed spun from a memorial in San Antonio to a memorial in Amarillo, from sorting the house to selling the house, from paperwork to probate court. God sprinkled His graces along the way that included notes, phone calls, and visits from friends as well as a miraculous gift: my family's four Bibles and prayer journals were clean while the rest of the car's contents were covered in oil. Eventually, life settled back down to reveal that death adds weight—weight to remember and to be remembered.

Memories hang like large millstones around your neck and weigh you down. These millstones of memory crop up in a variety of shapes and sizes in the forms of grumbling, nostalgia, bitterness, regret, shame, as well as future fears of futility and insignificance. Through God's mercy, He removes these heavy *millstones* and transforms them into *milestones*. These milestones serve as pillars of faith to glorify Him. Through His mercy, He redeems you out of misery. The miseries of memory are many, but His mercies abound even more. This book walks through the process of the redemption of memory from *millstones* to *milestones*.

For a starting point, the theological and scientific framework for memory will begin with the definition, importance, origins, and purpose of memory. These concepts march into the depths of memory right from the start, but a foundation is best established from these depths.

WHAT IS MEMORY?

Defining memory remains elusive, perhaps due to its constant employment. Memory operates unnoticed until it begins to fail (like in dementia). The human memory requires no on and off switch or manual to operate. Webster's Dictionary defines memory by its function, to retain and recollect.[1] Similarly, science defines memory as a cognitive system with a focus again on functions such as encoding, storing, and retaining information over periods of time.[2] When asking a typical person to define memory, many might think of studying for tests in school or in trying to find lost car keys. These definitions all collectively focus on the functions of memory but fall short in truly defining the essence of memory. In an attempt to further define memory, here are three categories to help: a gift, a craft, and a marvel.

Memory is a gift
• •

God created many living creatures with memory, but human memory functions at a higher level than the rest of terrestrial creation. Despite the universal and innate nature of memory among humans, uniqueness and diversity exist as humans possess different strengths in memory. The universal gift manifests unique talent. Consider movie maven Mary who, years later, recalls precise plot details from a single movie viewing; or music man Martin who hears a song in a department store that he replicates on the piano at home later that day; or master mechanic Mark who rebuilt an engine from one look at a diagram. Mary, Martin, and Mark each utilize memory, but in unique ways.

1 "memory," Merriam-Webster, 2020, Web. 24 August, 2020, www.merriam-webster.com.

2 Scott Young, "The Complete Guide to Memory," accessed 24 August, 2020, scottyoung.com, Feb. 2019.

Memory is a craft

Remembering is a craft.[3] Memory involves much more than the dictionary definition of function like *retain* and *recollect*. Memory is a creative function of the mind that deeply involves the will and emotions. The active memory draws upon the will and emotions to produce action—actions like worship and obedience. Craft implies purpose, the purpose to grow and mature. In discussing memory in the ancient world, Joshua Foer, the 2006 USA memory champion, agrees that "a trained memory wasn't just about gaining easy access to information, it was about strengthening one's personal ethics and becoming a more complete person."[4] Memory is not just a recorder to be replayed. It surpasses simple retention and recollection as it employs a craft that draws upon the emotions and will to bring about maturity.

Memory is a marvel

Memory is a creative marvel. Augustine captured this wonder when he muses,

> Men marvel at the mountain heights, the huge waves in the sea, the circuits of the stars, but they neglect to marvel at themselves. They do not marvel at the fact that while I was speaking of all these things, I was not looking at them with my own eyes. Yet I could never have spoken of them if I had not stored them within my memory, just as though I were looking at them outside.[5]

Augustine recognized that a common task of memory is truly miraculous. Pause and picture in your mind oceans, mountains, or stars; and then recognize memory just made those images come to life.

To add to the marvel, neuroscientists calculate the human brain

3 Mary Carruthers, *The Craft of Thought* (Cambridge University Press, 2000), 9.

4 Joshua Foer, *Moonwalking with Einstein* (Penguin Books, 2012), 110.

5 Augustine of Hippo, *Augustine's Confessions* (Sovereign Grace Publishers, 1971), 90.

contains around eighty-six billion neurons.[6] Under a microscope, each neuron resembles a tree with branches (called dendrites) and roots (called axons) interconnected with each other. Each single neuron makes over one thousand connections to other neurons with a total estimate of around one quadrillion connections (a 1 followed by 15 zeros) in the brain.[7] This interwoven neuronal forest of the human brain inspires images of the Amazon rain forest, the largest forest on earth with around 390 billion trees.[8] For comparison, four human brains of neurons equal one Amazon rainforest of trees. The wonder extends beyond sheer numbers.

If the number of neurons was the only determinant of the power of memory, a few select animals like the elephant would surpass the power of human memory since the elephant possesses three times the number of neurons than humans.[9] However, 98 percent of the elephant's neurons reside in the part of the brain called the cerebellum that controls the trunk of the elephant.[10] Unlike those of the elephant, human neurons are densely located in the cortex, the part of the brain that involves high-level thinking. The higher number of neurons in the cortex produces a higher function of memory compared to all other creatures. Just like in real estate, location matters, not just numbers. Human memory is well constructed by the Creator.

Human memory is difficult to define. Memory is universal and innate to humans but also unique to each individual. Beyond the functions of retention and recollection, a person uses memory to interact with the emotions and will for the purpose of maturity. Memory elicits marvel. Consider, memory requires memory to even define itself; and memory remembers that it forgets.[11]

6 Frederico A. C. Azevedo et al, "Equal numbers of neuronal and nonneuronal cells make the human brain an isometrically scaled-up primate brain," *The Journal of comparative neurology* vol. 513,5 (2009), 532–41.

7 Thomas M. Bartol et al, "Nanoconnectomic upper bound on the variability of synaptic plasticity," *eLife* vol. 4 e10778. 30 November, 2015.

8 Hans ter Steege et al, "Hyperdominance in the Amazonian tree flora," *Science* 342, 1243092 (2013).

9 Suzana Herculano-Houzel et al, "The elephant brain in numbers," *Frontiers in neuroanatomy* vol. 8 46 (12 June, 2014).

10 Ibid.

11 Augustine of Hippo, *Augustine's Confessions* (Sovereign Grace Publishers, 1971), 93.

HOW DOES MEMORY WORK?

During medical school, my wife and I headed to Uganda as part of an elective to work in rural and urban hospitals. The experience opened my eyes to the needs of the people but also the resourcefulness of the medical community. For a weekend escape, our host family took us to a national park. Our vehicle followed a calm elephant herd until one large elephant charged when we crept in a little too close. Humans might possess more intelligence, but elephants surpass us in body mass.

Many other animals wandered the plains freely, including giraffes we spotted snacking on acacia trees. I was surprised to discover this acacia tree snack provided an example of how neurons work. These acacia trees actually communicate with each other through the air. As a giraffe munches on the acacia leaves, the leaves release ethylene gas.[12] The ethylene gas signals neighboring trees of danger, and these trees pump toxins into their leaves, which make giraffes sick. The giraffes then will eat upwind to avoid these toxic leaves of downwind-neighboring trees. This communication by trees is simple compared to the vastly complex human brain signals that trigger neighbor neurons to respond.

Encode, store, retrieve
••••••••••••••••••••••••••••

Memory requires the human brain to encode, store, and retrieve. Science offers rudimentary explanations for how memory works; but in large part, the mechanisms of memory remain mysterious. Under a microscope, a neuron looks like an acacia tree. An axon wrapped in a myelin sheath is like the trunk wrapped in bark. At the top of one axon, up to one hundred thousand dendrites spread out like branches. At the bottom, axonal terminals look like tree roots.[13] Neurons communicate by transmitting electrical and chemical signals down their axonal trunks. The signal reaches the end of the axon where a space separates neurons called a synapse. Like the ethylene gas of the acacia tree, neurotransmitters (chem-

12 Richard Grant, "Do trees talk to each other?", March 2018, 24 August, 2020, smithsonianmag.com.

13 Bruce Alberts, *Essential Cell Biology*. 3rd ed. (Garland Science, 2009), 409.

icals) are then released that cross the synapse to communicate to the other neurons a positive or negative message. Then, the neighboring neuron that receives the message either continues to pass along this message at 200 miles per hour or puts a stop to it. Neurons not only send information, but certain parts of the brain encode and store a vast amount of information. A sample of the cortex of a human brain the size of a grain of sand holds an estimated 2,000 terabytes of information, enough data to "rival the entire digital content of today's world."[14] The hippocampus, a structure of the brain about the size of two shelled pecans with the appearance of a seahorse, plays the central role in memory. Without the hippocampus, memory does not exist.

WHY IS MEMORY IMPORTANT?

In "The Lost Mariner," Dr. Oliver Sacks, a British neurologist known for his detailed case studies of his clinical experiences, wrote an essay about Jimmie who suffered from an inability to form new memories.[15] Dr. Sacks met Jimmie when he was transferred to the Home for the Aged in 1975. Jimmie still recalled vividly his late adolescent life as a sailor in the Navy and still believed the year to be 1945. Despite vivid memories of submarines, shipmates, and Morse code, Jimmie lacked awareness of his memory's poor condition. In one account, when shown his own face in a mirror, terror seized him as he was shocked to see an old man staring back at him. A few minutes later, Jimmie forgot about the whole terrifying incident.

Jimmie struggled to perform daily tasks and develop relationships. Heartbroken for his patient, Dr. Sacks described him as "isolated in a single moment of being with a moat of forgetting all around him." Dr. Sacks asked for help from another physician, Dr. Luria. Dr. Luria, a Russian neuropsychologist, diagnosed Jimmie with Korsakoff Syndrome (a deficiency in a vitamin called thiamine), but Dr. Luria also encouraged Dr. Sacks to continue to care for Jimmie as "a man does not consist

14 Alison Abbott, "Neuroscience: Solving the brain," *Nature.* 499, 272–274. 18 July, 2013.

15 Oliver Sacks, *The Man Who Mistook His Wife for a Hat and Other Clinical Tales* (Harper and Row, *1987), 23–42.*

of memory alone." In discussing the importance of memory, a balance exists. Memory is important, but to what extent does it make up a man's identity? Is a man just the sum of his memories?

Memory is a cornerstone but not the essence of identity

Jeffrey Arthurs notes, "If we have no memory, we are adrift, because memory is the mooring to which we are tied."[16] The moorings of memory provide meaning to life. Kevin Horsley, a grandmaster of memory, believes the importance of memory goes even further as it serves as "the cornerstone of our existence."[17] Memory actively shapes the human core and habits. You are what you think (Prov. 23:7), and you think on what you remember. So, does memory determine your very identity?

Jonathan Edwards, an eighteenth-century preacher and theologian, argued that identity goes beyond just memory to the divine establishment of a unique soul for each human being.[18] Two unique beings might be given the same memory but would still have two separate souls who know nothing of each other's sufferings and joys.[19] The soul made in the image of God surpasses memory alone. Memory provides moorings and cornerstones for how you experience and interpret the world but falls short of fully defining your identity. Memory is important, but memory is not the sole essence of identity.

Memory is important in the Bible

The importance of memory also reverberates through the Bible with the extensive mention of memory throughout. In the Old Testament, the common root for remember, *zakar*, occurs 222 times.[20] The frequency of memory continues in the New Testa-

16 Jeffrey Arthurs, *Preaching as Reminding* (InterVarsity Press, 2017), 1.

17 Kevin Horsley, *Unlimited Memory* (TCK Publishing, 2013), 22.

18 Jonathan Edwards, *The Mind* www.apuritansmind.com, Note 72, Web. 24 August, 2020.

19 Ibid.

20 Eugene H. Merrill, "Remembering: A central theme in Biblical worship," *JETS vol.* 43 1 (March 2000), 28.

ment in the form of a Greek root *mneme* that gives rise to the English word for memory. Derivatives of these Greek words pop up in the majority of the New Testament books. The theme of memory pervades the pages of Scripture from start to finish. You might not see a specific word like "memory" or "remember" every time; but like the smell of orange blossoms carried by a spring breeze, you know the orange tree is nearby even when you do not see it. Just walk a few steps around the corner and you will find yourself in the shade of the blossoming tree. The aroma of remembrance wafts from the turning of the pages of Scripture.

HOW DID MEMORY ORIGINATE?

In my childhood backyard, the raised garden beds sat right next to the porch. In Texas, the hardened clay soil required extra preparation and enrichment that included shoveling horse manure into these garden beds on Saturday mornings with my dad. My mom loved to garden. I grew up with fresh, deep-red Texas tomatoes every summer. I would slice one and sprinkle some salt on it for an afternoon snack.

In gardening, my mom taught me the wonder of seeds. I would hold out my cupped hands while she carefully poured a few for me to push an inch under the ground. No biologist in the world truly understands how a seed grows into a vegetable or fruit-producing plant (my kids like to remind me that a tomato is a fruit and not a vegetable). Surprisingly, growth existed outside our "prepared" raised beds as small pecan trees would push up through the cracked, dry earth—a miracle that growth could occur in those harsh conditions.

To analyze the origins of the backyard pecan tree, examine its seed. Dig up a small seedling and see the tender green stem rising upward from the pecan with an equally long root pushing downward. If this seedling originated from a pecan that fell from our twenty-year-old pecan tree, where did that mature pecan tree originate from? Eventually, cycling back generations, the inquisitive will ask, "How did life originate—not just for plants— but for all life, including human beings and thus human memory?"

God is the primary cause of all things

All good origins originate from the Originator, God Himself. God is the primary cause of the universe full of His good effects (John 1:3; Rom. 11:36). Moses wrote, "Before the mountains were born or You gave birth to the earth and the world, even from everlasting to everlasting, You are God (Ps. 90:2). God exists completely independent of all things (1 Cor. 8:6, Acts 17:25), and His existence precedes and encompasses all things. "His duration is endless as His essence is boundless."[21] God is the Alpha and Omega (Rev. 1:8).

The simplicity of God

Since God is the fountain of all good things, His perfect memory serves as the starting point for understanding the origin of human memory. For God's memory to be perfectly complete, His essence and character must be perfect and complete. How can our imperfect minds discuss the perfect mind of God? We fall short. It is good to acknowledge that our conception of an incomprehensible God is incomplete—but this should not squelch our motivation to know Him more and more.

To discuss God, our feeble efforts require us to break things down into categories like communicable attributes of love and holiness (attributes human beings can have) and noncommunicable attributes like omniscience and omnipresence (attributes that belong only to God). Despite categorizing these attributes like separate slices of a pizza, God is free of all divisions and parts.[22] No attribute is more important than another.[23] This doctrine is called simplicity, and yet it is the farthest thing from simple. Simplicity spells out the mystery that God is holy (1 Peter 1:16) and God is love (1 John 4:8) in entirety without conflict. Simplicity dwells in unity. The scope of God's perfect memory involves all His attributes; but emphasis will be placed here on His omniscience and omnipresence.

21 Stephen Charnock, *Discourses upon the Existence and Attributes of God* (London: Thomas Tegg, 1840), 176.

22 Wayne Grudem, *Systematic Theology* (Zondervan, 1994), 178–79.

23 Ibid.

The omniscience of God
....

God's is omniscient; He is all-knowing. God "has no need to learn. But it is more: it is to say that God has never learned and cannot learn."[24]

This doctrine about God finds basis in how God has revealed Himself to us, in His Word. In Psalm 139:1–6 the psalmist pleads,

> O Lord, You have searched me and known me. You know when I sit down and when I rise up; You understand my thoughts from afar. You scrutinize my path and my lying down, and are intimately acquainted with all my ways. Even before there is a word on my tongue, Behold, O Lord, You know it all. You have enclosed me behind and before, and laid Your hand upon me. Such knowledge is too wonderful for me; it is too high, I cannot attain to it.

The psalmist expresses astonishment at the unreachable heights of God's vast knowledge. God knows even our invisible thoughts. "Nothing is more close and quick than thought; it is always unknown to others and often unobserved even by ourselves. Though my thoughts be ever so foreign and distant from one another, God understands the chain of them, and can distinguish their connection when so many of them slip my own notice I myself cannot put them together."[25] God knows the chain of your thoughts even now as you incompletely contemplate His omniscience.

Henry Ward Beecher provides this analogy: "Before men, we stand like opaque bee hives. Men can see the thoughts like bees that go in and out of us by actions and words but cannot tell what goes on inside the hive. Before God, we are like glass bee hives, and all that goes on inside he perfectly sees and understands."[26] The analogy may extend further. For God knows not just what

24 A. W. Tozer, *The Knowledge of the Holy* (HarperCollins, 1961), 55.

25 Matthew Henry, *Matthew Henry's Commentary,* vol. 3, "Psalm 139" (MacDonald Publishing Company, 1980), 756.

26 Augusta Moore, *Notes from Plymouth Pulpit: A Collection of Memorable Passages from the Discourses of Henry Ward Beecher* (New York: Derby and Jackson, 1859), 57.

goes on inside the hive but created the hive and knows the path and intention of each individual bee. "God without confusion, beholds as distinctly the actions of every man, as if that man were the only created being, and the Godhead were solely employed in observing him."[27] How boundlessly personal is God's mind!

The omnipresence of God

The limitless omniscience of God relates to His omnipresence, that "God fills every space with His entire being."[28] For God to know the path and intention of each bee, He must be present as the bee zigs and zags its path to the grove of blossoming trees. David links omniscience to omnipresence when he continues in Psalm 139,

> Where can I go from Your Spirit? Or where can I flee from Your presence? If I ascend to heaven, You are there; If I make my bed in Sheol, behold, You are there. If I take the wings of the dawn, If I dwell in the remotest part of the sea, even there Your hand will lead me, and Your right hand will lay hold of me. If I say, "Surely the darkness will overwhelm me, and the light around me will be night," even the darkness is not dark to You, and the night is as bright as the day. Darkness and light are alike to You.

As David makes clear, you cannot play hide-and-seek with God. God is in all places. He transcends the confines of space. The Maker is not limited by the space that He has made. "God is neither shut up in any place, nor shut out from any place."[29] God is immense.

Omnipresence and omniscience imply God does not "remember" in the same way that human beings remember, since human memory operates in the parameters of time and space. The Word of God uses the language of God's remembrance and

27 Henry Kirk White, "Omnipresence," *The Pilgrim or Monthly Visitor,* vol. 1 (New Haven: A. H. Maltby, 1822), 430.

28 Louis Berkhof, *Systematic Theology* (Banner of Truth Trust, 1949), 61.

29 Edward Leigh, *A Treatise of Divinity,* vol. 2 (London: E. Griffin for William Lee, 1647), 36.

forgetfulness "as a gracious concession on His part—the Infinite accommodating Himself to the language of the finite."[30] His condescension in anthropomorphic language gives the human mind a glimpse into His greatness.

The self-remembrance of God

The omniscient and omnipresent God's eternal memory operates perfectly on the basis of His own self-remembrance. The psalmist writes, "He has remembered His lovingkindness and His faithfulness to the house of Israel; all the ends of the earth have seen the salvation of our God" (Ps. 98:3). God's redemption arises from the remembrance of Himself, His lovingkindness, and His faithfulness. God remembers through the fountain of His own perfections. Join the psalmist in praising the Lord with a new song for the wonders He has done.

Creation of memory: A result of God's goodness

God's perfect memory provides the origins for man's memory. God's memory directly connects to human memory through creation. The first verse of Genesis establishes God's creator rights and ultimate authority. In Genesis 1:3, the Word of God created with the first words recorded, "Let there be light!" Light emanated forth from the Father of Lights! "The efficient cause and fountain, from whence all things originate"[31] spoke, and it was good. Creation resulted in goodness because God is good and revealed His perfect wisdom as "the master workman" (Prov. 8:30). Therefore, God did not create to add to Himself since perfection has no deficiency. Nothing is missing from God (Acts 17:25). A jewel that glitters in the sun does not add to the sun's brightness but shines by reflecting the sun's brightness.[32] Memory is a glittering jewel that reflects but does not outshine the Creator.

30 A. W. Pink, "Remembering," Web. 24 August, 2020, monergism.com.
31 Jonathan Edwards, "A dissertation concerning the end for which God created the world," Web. 24 August, 2020, monergism.com.
32 Ibid.

Creation of memory: The reflection of God

As the creation account rhythmically moved through day and night, a pivotal moment occurred when "God created man in His own image, in the image of God He created him" (Gen. 1:27a). God distinguished man as a unique reflection with image-bearing qualities of Himself, so much so that His own Son would descend to earth in the "likeness of men" (Phil. 2:7). Man possesses unique qualities like a soul and moral conscience that reflect God's image; but God also created Adam with a unique memory, an image-bearing quality that reflects God's perfect memory. Human memory, housed in spongy gray-and-white matter, remarkably demonstrates the profundity of our God. In other words, the mysterious depth of human memory hints at the measureless depths of the mind of God.

WHAT IS THE PURPOSE OF MEMORY?

Primary purpose: to glorify and worship God

The chief purpose of memory is to bring glory to God. Just as God is the first cause and beginning of all things, "He is the last, final cause for which they are made."[33] The first cause in creation is connected to the final cause and ultimate purpose, the glory of God (Rom. 11:36; Col. 1:16). As God is the fountain from which all things spring, so He is the ocean into which all worship will flow.[34] All creation brings glory to God, or God would not have created it.

Glorifying and enjoying God finds expression in worship, and worship implies worthiness of the object of worship. Eugene Merrill observes, "It is because God remembers that those who worship Him can recall His past and present benefits with full knowledge that the object of their devotion is reliable and therefore worthy of their implicit trust."[35] The believer's worship requires

33 Ibid.

34 John Howe, "I want to be yours," *Piercing Heaven: Prayers of the Puritans,* ed. Robert Elmer (Lexham Press, 2019), 178.

35 Eugene H. Merrill, "Remembering: A central theme in Biblical worship," *JETS* vol. 43 1 (March 2000), 30.

God's self-remembrance, and His self-remembrance makes Him worthy of worship. His self-remembrance frees the worshiper to remember self less. Worship "is inconceivable without knowing (remembering) who God is and what he has done on behalf of his people."[36] Worship mines memory and draws upon the riches stored up in the mind.

Dominion on the earth

The Genesis account establishes the primary purpose of human memory and also the secondary uses of memory prior to the entry of sin into the world. First, God established man's superior position over creation as He called man to "be fruitful and multiply, and fill the earth, and subdue it; and rule over the fish of the sea and over the birds of the sky and over every living thing that moves on the earth" (Gen. 1:28). Among other things, the superiority of human memory places man in a position of dominion over all other creation on earth. Human memory provides the capability of language, ingenuity, adaptation, and aptitude that rises above any other living creature on the planet. Without memory, humans would not subdue; they would be subdued.

The work of cultivation

Next, God employed man to cultivate and keep the garden (Gen. 2:15). Man's position of dominion informs his practice of work and service, which also depend on memory. In general, any job involves step-by-step tasks. Without memory, even a simple task erodes into a disorienting impossibility. Memory connects the initial step with a subsequent step. For basic garden cultivation, the simplest tasks like harvesting fruit from a tree would be impossible without memory. Likely, you would never even start, as you would need to first identify that the fruit is ripe and ready to pick. You would need to remember how to pick fruit and then where to place the picked fruit—in a basket or in your mouth. Memory initiates work as it supplies the basis for why you are working in the first place.

36 Ibid. p. 28.

The work of naming and organization

Naming and organizing is a function of memory. As a gardener, Adam worked as the first naming specialist. For those who endured biology in high school, recall the amount of mental effort to remember all the nomenclature (naming) involved in classifying by domain, kingdom, phylum, class, order, family, genus, and species. The animal kingdom contains over 1.6 million species.[37] Names help to organize and associate but also demonstrate creativity. In our family, one of the joys of a new pet is to choose the name. One of our first pets, a beta fish, was named "Owl" by our toddler. Now with older children, the puppy name options span from candylike Lollipop to nineteenth-century lady names like "Mabel." These names all popped into our minds due to associations. Think now about how Adam named animals with minimal to no association or experience. What an explosion of creative language! Adam not only named but had to remember the name he chose for each creature.

Obedience

The Genesis account also illustrates another purpose of uncorrupted human memory—obedience to God's commands. "The LORD God commanded the man, saying, 'From any tree of the garden you may eat freely; but from the tree of the knowledge of good and evil you shall not eat, for in the day that you eat from it you will surely die'" (Genesis 2:16–17). God gave the command with the supposition that Adam had the capacity to remember and obey. For Eve to be expected to obey, God or Adam had to teach her the command as well. Once God gave the command, the responsibility rested on the recipient to obey. Obedience flows out of right remembrance.

---

37 Zhi-Oiang Zhang, "Animal biodiversity: An outline of higher-level classification and survey of taxonomic richness (Addenda 2013)," *Zootaxa* vol. 3703 (2013), 1–82.

Relationship
······················

Finally, memory builds, maintains, and deepens relationships. In the garden, God constituted the penultimate human covenant of relationship in marriage between Adam and Eve as "they shall become one flesh." Any human relationship would not exist without memory. Memory binds together. Memory is not just what is connected by synapses but is what connects us to others and ultimately what connects us to God. Adam and Eve walked in the garden with God. God gifted man with memory, and memory potentiates a rich relationship and communion with Him.

God created the human memory for the primary purpose of glorifying and worshiping Him. In the garden, Adam and Eve fulfilled this purpose through dominion over creation, work, obedience, and relationship. Uncorrupted man dwelt with the incorruptible God.

Summary

The road map to the redemption of memory began with the definition and progressed to answer questions about memory: How does it work, why is it important, where does it originate, and what is its purpose? The road map for memory started with God as the origin and ended with God as the purpose. So why do we get so lost along the way?

Chapter 1
Application Questions

1.   After reading the first chapter, how would you define memory? How does this compare to before reading this chapter?

2.   Imagine life without memory. What would you miss the most? How would this change your life? How would this influence your identity?

3.   Read Psalm 139:1–12 and reflect on the impact of God's omniscience and omnipresence. Does this passage draw out hope or fear? Why?

4.   What is the primary purpose of human memory? Does this surprise you?

5.   What role has memory played in past relationships with God and others?

2

The Malady of Memory

My childhood backyard sloped up from the pecan tree to the mesquite tree that sat on the top of the hill. On a humid summer day, I climbed into the mesquite tree to enjoy the solitude of my treehouse. My dad had built the treehouse and cautioned me to be careful about exploring too far or high as mesquite branches are fairly brittle. However, occasionally I would look for a new place to sit. On this particular day, I climbed higher than usual to enjoy the view across my neighborhood and catch an afternoon breeze. Stepping on fragile branches designed for birds and not boys, I lifted my head above the treetop. Crack. Down I fell, grasping for anything to break my plunge to the earth. When I hit the ground, I sat with broken branches strewn all around me—but thankfully no broken bones in me.

THE GARDEN OF EDEN

My fall from the mesquite tree loosely parallels man's fall in the garden. In the garden of Eden, man attempted to climb and lift his head above his created station to be equal to his Creator and lay claim to deity. Man reached above his intended position and crashed to the ground.

The Temptation

In Genesis 3, the narrative introduces another creature, the crafty serpent that "the LORD God had made" who speaks to Eve. The serpent twisted a positive command by God that Adam and Eve may eat freely from any tree of the garden into a negative command: "Indeed, has God said, 'You shall not eat from any tree of the garden?'" Now, through the rephrasing of the positive command into a negative question, the temptation began to bend Eve toward self and away from God. Satan craftily fed subtle misinformation to suggest lies about God and His goodness.

The Fall

Eve answered the serpent that "...from the fruit of the garden we may eat" (Hebrew *'akal*). Eve subtracted from God's command to eat freely (Hebrew *'akal 'akal*). Then Eve continued in her answer that "...from the fruit of the tree which is in the middle of the garden, God has said, 'You shall not eat or touch it or you will die.'" Eve adds "touch" to the original command. Finally, she softened the consequence of disobedience from "surely die" (Hebrew *muwth muwth*), to "die" (Hebrew *muwth*). Eve's memory was created and declared good, but her memory of the command succumbed to an external twisting temptation. Eve reconstructed God's commands with removal of the command's freedom, addition of restrictions, and softening of its consequence.

The serpent tempted Eve to doubt God's goodness as "God knows that in the day you eat from it your eyes will be opened, and you will be like God, knowing good and evil." The external enticement angled Eve away from her good and wise Creator and toward herself, a good but subordinate, created being. Essentially, Eve forgot the character of her Creator. She doubted. No longer delighting in her Creator, she reached out for the fruit of delight and ate. Eve then approached Adam with the fruit, and Adam took the fruit from Eve's hand instead of taking her hand and endeavoring to lead her to repentance.

THE CORRUPTION OF HUMAN MEMORY

What happened in the garden did not stay in the garden. The first sin brought death and disorder into the world that affects all mankind with a corruption of the mind and memory (Titus 1:15). Anthony Burgess, a Puritan preacher, writes: "It is from the pollution of the memory that all wickedness is committed."[1] Burgess notes there is a twofold weakness of memory: First, "a natural weakness which arises from the constitution of the body" like dementia or other ailments that are an effect of a fallen world but not sin itself, and second, "a moral forgetfulness of 'holy duties.'"[2] Due to its corruption, memory no longer operates as God designed it. Rather than glorifying and enjoying God, man now distorts memory to glorify and enjoy self.

The blinding effects of sin

Through the fall of Adam, every human inherits a sin nature (Rom. 5:12–13). The sin nature corrupts not just your heart but also your mind. "No human exists and indeed no human faculty exists which is exempt from sin's effects, and therefore it is impossible to identify, in a way which is itself undistorted by sin's effects, exactly where the noetic (mental) effects of sin are present."[3] In other words, the deceitful, pervasive depth of the sin nature makes identification of these sinful effects difficult.

To clarify, common grace maintains the mind's ability to use reason, to search for knowledge, and to recognize beauty and truth (Rom. 1:18–20). John Calvin, a French theologian and reformer, notes,

> Shall we deny that the truth shone upon the ancient jurists who established civic order and discipline with such great equity? Shall we say that the philosophers were blind in their fine observation and artful description of nature? What shall we say of all the mathematical sciences? Shall we

1 Anthony Burgess, *The Extent of Original Sin in Every Faculty of the Soul,* Web. 24 August, 2020, monergism.com, 82.

2 Ibid. p. 85

3 Stephen K. Moroney, *The Noetic Effects of Sin* (Lexington Books, 1999), 80.

consider them the ravings of madmen? No, we cannot read the writings of the ancients on these subjects without great admiration.[4]

In other words, despite its corruption, the mind still possesses abilities. However, the mind on its own is blinded "from seeing the light of the gospel" (2 Cor. 4:3–4) unless the mind is regenerated by God's saving grace (Eph. 2:8–9). Man cannot correctly diagnose and redeem himself from his fallen condition.

The self-deception of sin

To illustrate, humans possess little knowledge of what we truly look like. We recognize others' faces at a high level of precision but lack ability to recognize our own faces. In a panel discussion at the National Portrait Gallery in London, neuroscientist Dr. James Kilner noted that research suggests how poor we are at self-facial recognition. Researchers compiled a series of photos with an original photo of the participant and then a series of digitally altered photos.[5] The researchers asked the participants to pick the photo that most closely resembled them from this series of photos. The participants performed poorly and selected the digitally altered photo that made them appear younger and more attractive.[6]

The same concept applies to the state and condition of our minds. We select the better version of ourselves, the one that is more attractive. In essence, we do not truly understand who we are. "For if anyone is a hearer of the word and not a doer, he is like a man who looks at his natural face in a mirror; for once he has looked at himself and gone away, he has immediately forgotten what kind of person he was" (James 1:23–24). James identifies how quickly the mind forgets the flaws. English writer and philosopher, G. K. Chesterton, writes,

4 John Calvin, *Institutes of Christian Religion,* vol. 1, Book 2 (Westminster: John Knox Press, 2006), 274.

5 National Portrait Gallery (2014). *The Curated Ego: What Makes a Good Selfie?* 3 March, 2014, Web. 24 August, 2020.

6 Ibid.

We have all read ... the story of the man who has forgotten his name. This man walks about the streets and can see and appreciate everything; only he cannot remember who he is. Well, every man is that man in the story. Every man has forgotten who he is. One may understand the cosmos, but never the ego; the self is more distant than any star. Thou shalt love the Lord thy God; but thou shalt not know thyself. We are all under the same mental calamity; we have all forgotten our names. We have all forgotten what we really are.... we forget that we have forgotten.[7]

Awareness of our self-deception establishes an important step in the humble redemption of the mind and memory, the unveiling of its true identity. It is an important step to no longer deny the "indisputable dirt"[8] of our sin nature.

THE FAILURES OF HUMAN MEMORY

No one enjoys reflecting on failure. You won't visit a friend's house and find a trophy case filled with failures; and yet, the recognition of the failures of our lives pushes us to see our need for a remedy, a Savior. It is dangerous when we refuse to recognize our need for help.

A lady came to the emergency room by ambulance for leg wounds. Homeless and sad, she did not have much to say. I asked if I could examine her legs, and she nodded. Lifting back the sheet, the stench of rotting flesh wafted up; her legs were moving. By moving, I mean her flesh was crawling with maggots that were wiggling in and out, feasting on her dead flesh. After I recovered my composure and covered her moving legs, I told her that she had maggots, and her legs needed to be cleaned off and bandaged. Shockingly, she refused. She did not believe that she had maggots because she was blind. Just like this woman, we, too, are blinded by sin, our maggot-infested condition. Those who are well or think they are well do not seek out a doctor (Matt. 9:12).

7 G. K. Chesterton, *Orthodoxy* (Moody Publishers, 2009), 83.
8 Ibid. p. 28.

The corruption of memory
••••••••••••••••••••••••••••••••••

Sin corrupto memory. You forget what you should remember and remember what you should forget while doubting that God will forget what He promised and will remember what He promised to forget. Memory follows the fallen pattern observed by Martin Luther as *incurvatus in se*—"curved into ourselves."[9] The corruption of memory at the fall switches God's perfect memory with man's imperfect memory, the glory of God to the glory of self, and God at the center to man at the center.

Truly, memory is a gauge for what you value. What you remember reveals what is important, and what you forget shows what is unimportant. "It is really only those things to which we are indifferent, and which can thus shove to the very peripheries of our minds as irrelevant, which we are able to forget."[10] When it comes to sorting your memories into the treasure trove of importance or the trash heap of indifference, you collect junk and cast away jewels. Spurgeon says, "Memory is very treacherous about the best things; by a strange perversity engendered by the fall, it treasures up the refuse of the past and permits priceless treasures to lie neglected, it is tenacious of grievances and holds benefits all too loosely."[11] Memory malfunctions with a prioritization of the important over the unimportant. Instead of picking up a chisel to engrave the important, you pick up a piece of chalk. The important is erased while the unimportant is etched.

It is commonly believed that you only use ten percent of your brain, but this does not explain the dysfunction of memory. Dr. Barry Gordon dispelled this myth he thinks came "from people's conceptions about their own brains: they see their own shortcomings as evidence of the existence of untapped gray matter."[12] At rest you might use about ten percent of your brain, but every day you utilize one hundred percent of your brain. Dysfunction exists not from poor utilization but from pervasive fallenness.

9 Martin Luther, *Luther's Works*, vol. 25, 345.

10 Carl Trueman, "Lest we forget," *Themelios*, vol. 34.3, 285.

11 Charles H. Spurgeon, *The Treasury of David*, vol. 2, "Psalm 103." (Thomas Nelson Publishers, 1984), 276.

12 Robynne Boyd, "Do people only use 10 percent of their brains?", Web. 24 August, 2020, scientificamerican.com, 7 February, 2008.

Categories of memory failure

Human memory fails in two ways—omission and commission. Omission is a failure to conform and perform an action, forgetting the important. Commission is to transgress and perform the sinful action, remembering the unimportant. Corruption of memory involves both omission and commission. Daniel Schacter, a memory researcher at Harvard, divides the malfunctions of memory into the subcategories that include the omissions of transience, absentmindedness, blocking, and the commissions of bias, misattribution, and persistence.[13] Through a Biblical lens, these subcategories will be sifted to illuminate the dysfunctional nature of fallen memory.

TRANSIENCE: LOSS OF MEMORY OVER TIME

To begin, transience is the first failure in the category of omission. Transience refers to the loss of memory over time as neurons decay. "The amount we forget is much more impressive than the amount we remember."[14] By itself, the act of forgetting is not inherently sinful. However, forgetfulness invades areas of spiritual importance. Because of a sin nature, transience targets the spiritually important and "disturbs our thinking in some areas more than others."[15]

Forgetting God: who He is

First and foremost, you forget God. "Can a virgin forget her ornaments, or a bride her attire? Yet My people have forgotten Me days without number" (Jer. 2:32). Jeremiah highlights the connection of importance and remembrance. Forgetting God includes forgetting who He is. Hosea connects man's forgetfulness to God's omniscience and omnipresence. "And they do not consider in their hearts that I remember all their wickedness. Now their deeds are all around them; they are before My face" (Hos. 7:2). Human memory ironically forgets God's perfect memory. The psalmist

13 Daniel L. Schacter, *The Seven Sins of Memory* (Mariner Books, 2002).

14 Alan Baddeley, *Essentials of Human Memory* (Psychology Press, 2014), 152.

15 Stephen K. Moroney, *The Noetic Effects of Sin* (Lexington Books, 1999), 73.

picks up this connection when he recounts the sin of Israel as "they did not remember Your abundant kindnesses, but rebelled by the sea, at the Red Sea. Nevertheless, He saved them for the sake of His name, that He might make His power known" (Ps. 106:7–8). The psalmist recognized the need for the remembrance of God and His character in light of the history of His people's forgetfulness of God.

Forgetting God: what He has done

The psalmist also connects forgetfulness to what God has done. "They quickly forgot His works; They did not wait for His counsel, but craved intensely in the wilderness, and tempted God in the desert" (Ps. 106:13-14). "They forgot God their Savior, who had done great things in Egypt, wonders in the land of Ham and awesome things by the Red Sea" (Ps. 106:21–22). The people of Israel forgot their deliverance from slavery in Egypt by the mighty hand of God in the plagues and parting of the Red Sea. How often do you do the same with God, forget who He is and forget what He has done? Just as Israel forgot their salvation in the Exodus, so you forget your salvation in Christ who freed you from the bondage of sin.

Forgetting God: what He has commanded

Transience carries over from forgetting God to forgetting His commandments. If you neglect and forget God, you will also naturally neglect and forget His commandments. Moses joins these together when he warns, "Beware that you do not forget the Lord your God by not keeping His commandments and His ordinances and His statutes which I am commanding you today" (Deut. 8:11). Moses equates forgetfulness of the Lawgiver with disobedience to the Law. Jeremiah gives a glimpse into the reason why you forget God's commandments and oracles (prophecies) when he writes, "For you will no longer remember the oracle of the LORD, because every man's own word will become the oracle, and you have perverted the words of the living God, the LORD of hosts, our God" (Jer. 23:36). You replace God's commands with your own commands.

Forgetting God: fixating on self

Transience subverts your memory away from the important things of God and fixates on self. My words replace God's words. Raising self above God depends on forgetting your position, who you are, and where you came from. Ezekiel 16 creates vivid imagery of Israel's origins. God raised up Israel from an unloved and lowly state abandoned in an open field "squirming in your blood" (Ezek.16:5–6). After God rescued and blessed her as His own daughter, Israel trusted in her own beauty and acted wickedly because she "did not remember the days of [her] youth, when [she was] naked and bare and squirming in [her] blood" (Ezek. 16:22). Transience erases humble origins. Transience also decays the memory traces of sin to where you declare yourself innocent; and yet ignorance is not innocence (1 Cor. 4:4). In transience, ignorance soothes the soul while the soul is feasted upon by maggots.

ABSENTMINDEDNESS: DISTRACTION FROM THE IMPORTANT

Omission in memory involves absentmindedness. Absentmindedness is distraction that diverts from the important. In transience, memory erodes over time; while in absentmindedness, memory never forms and consolidates due to distraction. "If you have no attention, you have no retention."[16] Distraction is the greatest enemy of memory.[17]

Distractions of technology

Distractions abound in the digital age. Phones operate based on distractions with notifications and alerts. Nicholas Carr writes,

> The influx of competing messages that we receive whenever we go online not only overloads our working memory; it makes it much harder for our frontal lobes to concentrate

16 Kevin Horsley, *Unlimited Memory* (TCK Publishing, 2013), 98.

17 Joshua Foer, "Feats of memory anyone can do," *TED, Feb. 2012,* www.ted.com/talks/joshua_foer_feats_of_memory_anyone_can_do.

our attention on any one thing. The process of memory consolidation can't even get started. And, thanks once again to the plasticity of our neuronal pathways, the more we use the Web, the more we train our brain to be distracted—to process information very quickly and very efficiently but without sustained attention. That helps explain why many of us find it hard to concentrate even when we're away from our computers. Our brains become adept at forgetting, inept at remembering.[18]

Distraction is dangerous. Distraction might bring to mind a whimsical image of a boy chasing a vibrant butterfly and yet distraction eventually leads to destruction as the boy plunges over the cliff. Absentmindedness diverts not just from remembering in general but from remembering the spiritually important things. The Bible commands you to listen up and pay attention so that you do not drift away (Heb. 2:1).

Distractions of prosperity

Distractions abound beyond technology, including prosperity. The Bible is filled with men like Demas who "loved this present world" and deserted Paul (2 Tim. 4:10). Wealth itself is not evil, and, in fact, may be the result of the blessings of faithfulness as in the case of Abraham, a rich man. Yet, Hosea warns, "As they had their pasture, they became satisfied, and being satisfied, their heart became proud; therefore they forgot Me" (Hos. 13:6). Prosperity can distract from the Giver and source of all good things and attract to the things of this world.

Deep-sea anglerfishes famously practice the art of allurement in the dark. These fish are shaped with a protrusion from their head that looks like a fishing pole with a neon lure attached to the end. The lure is called an *illicium*, a word with the Latin root meaning "to entice" or "mislead."[19] The fish wiggles the lure to attract and kill its prey. In life, the treasures of this world glow in the darkness and entice away from the

18 Nicholas Carr, *The Shallows: What the Internet is Doing to our Brains* (W. W. Norton and Company, 2010), 119.

19 Jonathan Balcombe, *What a Fish Knows.* Scientific American, 2017, 33.

true Light of the world, Jesus Christ. How easily does the mind wander away from the treasures of heaven to chase the trivialities of earth?

BLOCKING: INTERFERENCE IN RETRIEVAL

Blocking results from an inability to retrieve a memory due to interference as something gets in the way, despite a helpful cue. While absentmindedness distracts from forming memories, blocking interferes with retrieval of memories already stored.

Interference with idols from creation

With absentmindedness, "Satan disguises himself as the angel of light" to give the appearance of the Father of lights. Satan employs interference with the very creation that reflects the Creator. Isaiah provides a striking illustration of the man who "plants a fir, and the rain makes it grow" (Isa. 44:14). Planting and cultivating should draw your mind back to God. However, the man ignores the Creator and focuses on function as the tree provides wood to burn for warmth and to bake food (Isa. 44:15a). "Half of it he burns in the fire" (44:16a) and to the other half "he bows down and prays 'Deliver me, for you are my god (44:17b).'"

Isaiah finishes the illustration by pointing out that this man has a deceived heart and implores, "Remember these things, O Jacob, and Israel, for you are My Servant; I have formed you, you are My servant, O Israel, you will not be forgotten by Me. I have wiped out your transgressions like a thick cloud and your sins like a heavy mist. Return to me, for I have redeemed you" (Isa. 44:21-22). Observe that God reminds His people of His Creator rights and links to His redemptive power. Don't miss and even replace your Creator. "For even though they knew God, they did not honor Him as God or give thanks, but they became futile in their speculations, and their foolish heart was darkened" (Rom. 1:21).

In His original good design, God created memory to reflect His image and bring Him glory. But since sin has entered the world, the mirror of memory now loosely swings on a hinge that gets pulled by the inherent sin nature downward to reflect back on man himself and outward to idols, and yet rarely upward to His creator.

Interference with replacement of the Creator

In blocking, deception runs to the very depths of distortion. Calvin writes,

> For we know how reluctant man is to lower himself, in order to set other creatures above him. Therefore, when he chooses to worship wood and stone rather than be thought to have no God, it is evident how very strong this impression of a Deity must be; since it is more difficult to obliterate it from the mind of man, than to break down the feelings of his nature,—these certainly being broken down, when, in opposition to his natural haughtiness, he spontaneously humbles himself before the meanest object as an act of reverence to God.[20]

Blocking disrupts worship. You favor creation and forget the Creator. You focus on the tree but must remember the Creator of the tree, the One who hung on a tree to die for you and me.

Interference with idols of the mind

To clarify, idolatry runs much broader than the formation of physical idols from wood like the above illustration. It might be easy to dismiss idolatry as an ancient Middle Eastern problem, but idolatry is, more often, a construct of "the thoughts, desires, longings, and expectations that we worship in the place of the true God."[21] This definition acknowledges the broad scope of idols and their destructive power as they displace God from the center of worship. Idolatry pervades the mind not just in a trifling way. The blocking of idolatry steals worship (Jer. 18:15).

20 John Calvin, *Institutes of Christian Religion,* vol. 1, Book 1 (Bierton Particular Baptists, 2019), 62.

21 Elyse Fitzpatrick, *Idols of the Heart* (P&R Publishing, 2002), 23.

BIAS: ALTERATION OF A RECALLED MEMORY

Human memory fails, first of all, in omission, forgetting the important. Transience, absentmindedness, and blocking provided three categories to sort memory loss, how memory forgets the important. Consider the ways you remember, but remember wrongly, sins of commission. First, bias infiltrates your memory especially in reconstruction of the past. Many forms of bias exist, but the focus here will be on recall bias and confirmation bias.

Recall bias

Recall bias occurs when a memory is retrieved but is altered and incomplete from the original. The Pharisees demonstrate recall bias as they seek to prove Jesus is not the Messiah based on His city of origin. In their blindness, they first assume Jesus is from Galilee and miss His birthplace in Bethlehem (John 7:41–42). Then, the prejudice against Galilee perpetuates another error as they falsely claim that no prophet ever came from Galilee (John 7:52); and yet Jonah arises from Galilee 3 miles north of Nazareth in Gath-Hepher (2 Kings 14:25).

Prejudice and recall bias travel side by side, one never far from the other. The flounder begins its life like a normal upright fish with one eye on each side. As the flounder ages, a mysterious process takes place over a few days, and one eye migrates to join the other eye on one side of the body.[22] The flounder lives the rest of its life with one side of its body resting on the ocean floor while the other side faces up with two eyes peering around. So it is with prejudice and recall bias. One eye migrates towards the other and transforms your view of the world. You end up only seeing one side, with blindness to the other.

Confirmation bias

Confirmation bias creeps in to confirm and promote your presuppositions. You will modify new information to confirm and

22 Jonathan Balcombe, *What a Fish Knows.* Scientific American, 2017, 27.

promote that you are right, while ignoring anything to the contrary. Confirmation bias must be guarded against in medicine. It is common to anchor on to what you think might be going on with a patient and miss the true diagnosis.

A patient came to the ER for a sore throat that was very uncomfortable. The patient had already been seen by the primary doctor who had unsuccessfully treated her for strep throat. After reading the prior note with her story of two weeks of worsening throat pain without fever, I stepped into the room to examine the patient. I looked into her throat, which again was normal-appearing without any signs of infection. Moving quickly, I stepped out to see another patient that had arrived, unsure what else to do for her.

As I came back in to discuss a possible plan, the patient was reclining back in the gurney. Before even saying another word, I made the diagnosis. Her thyroid (the gland located at the front of the neck) was enlarged; the shadow from the overhead light now made it obvious. The diagnosis was Hashimoto's thyroiditis, inflammation of the thyroid when your immune system attacks itself. How was the diagnosis initially missed? The medical providers anchored on to the most common cause of sore throat, infection and particularly strep throat. The exam focused on the inside of the mouth while forgetting to examine the outside of the neck. With confirmation bias, you look all around to confirm you are right. You forget to look internally to your sinful condition and remember that you need help from the great Physician.

MISATTRIBUTION: ASSIGNMENT OF MEMORY TO THE WRONG SOURCE

The second way that memory remembers wrongly (commission) includes misattribution. Misattribution assigns a memory to the wrong source. In general, a corrupted memory attributes sin and other failings to others and attributes credit for accomplishments to ourselves.

Blame-shifting

1 Samuel 15 provides an excellent example of blame-shifting, a form of misattribution. God tasked Saul to punish the Amalekites,

descendants of Esau, because they had ruthlessly attacked Israel as they came out of Egypt (Ex. 17:8–16). God commanded Israel to remember what they did (Deut. 25:17–18), and God ordered Saul to utterly destroy them (1 Sam. 15:2–3). Following the battle with the Amalekites, Saul set up a monument for himself (1 Sam. 15:12), a claim to the credit for victory. Then, Samuel went to meet Saul. Saul recounted to Samuel his perceived obedience of God's command to utterly destroy everything; and yet, he had spared King Agag and the choicest spoils, "unwilling to destroy them utterly" (1 Sam. 15:9). Saul excused himself and misattributed the blame to the people for this disobedience (1 Sam. 15:21). Observe the intermingling of lying and blame-shifting. Lying creates an alternative reality that deceives to the point that memory may begin to retain the lie as truth.

Credit-shifting to others

In contrast to blame-shifting that misattributes failings to others, credit-shifting assigns credit for achievements to gods or self. The corrupted memory steals worship from God to direct it elsewhere. Look no further than the golden calf. God had just delivered the Israelites from bondage and defeated the gods of Egypt with the ten plagues, divided the Red Sea for Israel to cross, destroyed Pharaoh's army, and provided water, manna, and meat on the way to Mount Sinai. The Israelites, quaking, encountered God at Mount Sinai. They backed away in fear and asked Moses to mediate (Ex. 20:18–19). However, when Moses was "delayed" forty days on Mount Sinai, the people asked Aaron to "make us a god who will go before us" (Ex. 32:1).

Despite living in the shadow of Sinai in the presence of God, the people forgot their Deliverer and turned from holy dread to unholy disdain. Aaron instructed the people to tear off the gold rings, likely jewelry that was part of the plunder of the Egyptians, to craft an idol. While Mount Sinai smoked like a furnace (Ex. 19:18) from the presence of God, Aaron threw the gold into a furnace and fashioned the gold into a calf. Calvin writes, "The human mind is a perpetual forge of idols."[23] He goes on to explain,

23 John Calvin, *Institutes of Christian Religion*, vol.1, Book 1 (The Westminster Press, 1960), 108.

"The god whom man has thus conceived inwardly he attempts to embody outwardly. The mind, in this way, conceives the idol, and the hand gives it birth."[24]

The next day Israel celebrated the idol who "brought them up out of the land of Egypt" (Ex. 32:4)! In an illogical misattribution of credit, the people bring burnt offerings and worship the idol they just made for a past deliverance that predated the idol's very existence. God does not share worship with anyone or anything else, as nothing compares to Him. This misattribution of credit kindled God's anger. Moses entreated the Lord to "Remember Abraham, Isaac, and Jacob, and Israel, Your servants, whom You swore by Yourself...." (Ex. 32:13). God remembered His covenant while the people forgot God and His deliverance. Lest you assign this sin of memory to Israel only, how often do you mold idols in the flicker of the mind's furnace, while sitting in the presence of God?

Credit-shifting to self

Misattribution not only shifts credit for accomplishments to gods but also to self. King Hezekiah took credit for his wealth when the Babylonians visited. He showed off "all that is in my house; there is nothing among my treasuries that I have not shown them" (Isa. 39:4). Hezekiah did not credit God for his wealth that God preserved with the miraculous defeat of the Assyrians. Isaiah prophesied that "all that is in your house ... will be carried to Babylon; nothing shall be left" (2 Kings 20:17). Interestingly, the Babylonian King Nebuchadnezzar, who pillaged Hezekiah's treasures, also suffered from credit-shifting. "The king reflected and said, 'Is this not Babylon the great, which I myself have built as a royal residence by the might of my power and for the glory of my majesty?'" (Dan. 4:30). God humbled Nebuchadnezzar. The king went from the palace to a pasture, from eating grapes to eating grass. Then, the Babylonian king came to his senses and recognized "that the Most High is ruler over the realm of mankind and bestows it on whomever He wishes" (Dan. 4:32b). The glory shifted back to God.

---

24 Ibid.

Pride: inflation of self

The dysfunctional memories of these kings are just like ours: mangled by pride. Pride utilizes memory to inflate self and deflate God. The fragile ego is "in imminent danger of being deflated"[25] like an overinflated balloon. The imagery ties in well with the Greek word for conceit, *typhoo*, which means to be puffed up (1 Tim. 6:4). Like a blown-up balloon, pride carries you upward, ascending toward thoughts of equality with your Creator. But as pride puffs up the mind, it drags you lower along the ground; and you eat the dust from which you were made. "Whoever exalts himself shall be humbled" (Matt. 23:12a). No balloon stays inflated forever.

Pride: deflation of others

Pride not only attempts to positionally elevate you above God but also above others. C.S. Lewis observes,

Pride gets no pleasure out of having something, only out of having more of it than the next person. We say that people are proud of being rich, or clever, or good-looking, but they are not. They are proud of being richer, or cleverer, or better-looking than others. If everyone else became equally rich, or clever, or good-looking there would be nothing to be proud about.[26]

Pride manages the ledger of self-worth to debit and credit accordingly. Your prideful memory remembers another person's flaws and minimizes your own.

Pride: destruction of self

Truly, pride carries your mind to illogical heights of hubris. To illustrate, I will never forget a man who walked into the emergency room holding the back of his head with blood dripping down his neck, yelling that he had been shot. Quickly, we moved to the closest trauma room to assess and care for him. On initial observation, the man was walking and talking, a positive indication for

---

25 Tim Keller, *The Freedom of Self Forgetfulness* (10Publishing, 2012), 20.
26 C. S. Lewis, *Mere Christianity* (Macmillan Publishing, 1952), 109–110.

his overall well-being. Soon, the excitement settled down as it became clear that the bullet likely had not caused serious injury. An x-ray showed the bullet lodged against the skull without any entry into the brain or even a fracture of the skull as the bullet had slowed down when passing through the car exterior and seat. Once I delivered the good news to the patient, he stood up and began to strut around the room boasting to everyone around that he was the most amazing man with the hardest head. I agreed; the man displayed the hardest and most arrogant head I had ever seen. The man shifted credit for his survival to the hardness of his own skull. Similarly, credit-shifting from God to self demonstrates the level of corruption of the mind, willing to soar to heights of irrationality rather than honor God.

PERSISTENCE: PRESERVATION OF USELESS MEMORIES

Persistence focuses on the memories that are useless and should be forgotten but continue to linger. Every person's memory operates with a certain capacity to store but also easily retrieve. Clutter kills capacity and utility. If you remember everything, you are unable to distinguish useful from useless, leaving a cluttered mess of the useful buried underneath the useless. Persistence picks up the useless, and places it in a prominent position despite its purposelessness. Meanwhile, useful sits under the clutter, forgotten and untouched.

Attention to the meaningless

Paul exhorted Timothy to not "pay attention to myths and endless genealogies, which give rise to mere speculation rather than furthering the administration of God which is by faith" (1 Tim. 1:4). Paul advised Timothy to not give a prominent place to the unimportant and useless, especially to detriment of the central tenets of faith. The persistence of these myths was not just a distraction but a harm to the church.

Attention to the worthless

Paul also warned his readers not to turn back to the "weak and worthless elemental things, to which you desire to be enslaved all over again" (Gal. 4:9). The worthless and elemental things stick like Velcro to your memory while righteousness slips away from memory's fingers like a slimy salmon. "For memory grasps with an iron hand ill things but the good she holds with feeble fingers."[27] The worthless remains while the worthwhile slips away.

Summary

Memory corrupts in many different ways, both in failures of omission and commission. The corruption of the mind infects the core, disorients, and results in the exchange of what is important for what is unimportant. You forget what you should remember and remember what you should forget while doubting that God will forget what He promised and will remember what He promised to forget. This double distortion of memory does not cancel out but rather amplifies the problem.

The malady of memory often goes unnoticed like the maggots that infested the blind woman's legs. These maggots of transience, absentmindedness, blocking, bias, misattribution, and persistence squirm around feasting on flesh of the mind. This corruption not only blinds to diagnosis, but then, when discovered, tries to convince that it is not harmful but actually helpful. After all, maggots do help clean out dead tissue; but these maggots are part of the problem and not the solution. They devour and distort the mind toward self and away from God, the Great Physician. These maggots do not follow the principle to first do no harm, but rather inflict harm and hide the treatment.

27 Charles H. Spurgeon, "The carnal mind is enmity against God," 22 April, 1855, Web. 24 August, 2020, spurgeon.org.

Chapter 2
Application Questions

1. What way do you struggle most in remembering God?

2. What attribute of God do you find the easiest to forget? What attribute of God do you think on the most?

3. In what ways has technology helped or distracted your memory about spiritual things? Do you need to make any changes?

4. Are you aware of any idols that interfere with your memory? If so, what are they?

5. In relationships, did blame-shifting or credit-shifting play a role in a recent conflict? If your answer is yes, what did that look like?

3

The Cudgel of Corrupted Memory

In its original created form, the tree of memory was very good, elegant, and without sin. When man fell, these beautiful branches of memory broke off from the weight of the curse, in a way similar to my treehouse experience. You carry the broken branches of memories in your hand like a cudgel. A cudgel is an older English term for a club-shaped weapon. This imagery originated from John Bunyan's *The Pilgrim's Progress*[1] and used by Spurgeon in an 1865 sermon.[2] In the allegorical tale, Bunyan chronicles the story of Christian who journeys through life meeting different characters, both friend and foe, on his way to the Celestial City (heaven). In one scene, Christian and his friend, Hopeful, venture off the right path through a gate onto the soft grasses of By-Path meadow. Misled by the guide, Vain-Confidence, and caught in a rainstorm, the two pilgrims find shelter on the property of Giant Despair. The giant discovers them sleeping and locks them in the dungeon of Doubting Castle. The Giant beats the men with his cudgel—a cudgel formed from Christian

1 John Bunyan, *The Pilgrim's Progress* (London: Gall and Inglis, undated), 147–56.

2 Charles H. Spurgeon, "Memory: the handmaid of hope," 15 October, 1865, Web. 24 August, 2020, spurgeon.org.

and Hopeful's own merciless memories. These memories include regrets like their bad choice to leave the right road and their neglect of the warning to never wander off. These memories form a club that beat their minds and bodies. Continuing the downward spiral, the men bring to mind more of their past sins, until they begin to despair even of life itself. The effects of the cudgel of memory can be devastating.

You wield the cudgel of memory and distort the good and bad past to wound the present. The distortions revolve around comparisons of the present with the past. A distortion of your "good" past includes grumbling and nostalgia, while a distortion of a "bad" past consists of bitterness, regret, shame, and unrepentant guilt. These effects are not an exhaustive list but a starting point to begin to unravel the distortions of memory.

THE DISTORTIONS OF A GOOD PAST

Grumbling
....

Grumbling bubbles to the surface as a distortion of a good past. Grumblers exhibit the "brown grass complex." The brown grass complex concludes that all grass is greener than the grass you are currently standing on. Comparison breeds complaining. The sons of Israel arrived in the Wilderness of Sin (short for Sinai) and began to sin (Ex. 16). One month earlier, Israel had praised the Lord for victory over the Egyptians at the Red Sea, a mountaintop experience; but now they have descended into the canyon of complaining. The same lips that glorified God now grumble, "Would that we had died by the LORD's hand in the land of Egypt, when we sat by the pots of meat, when we ate bread to the full; for you have brought us out into this wilderness to kill this whole assembly with hunger" (Ex. 16:3).

Grumbling is used to direct fault toward others; in this case, the people grumbled against Moses, for leading them out of the slavery of Egypt into freedom. Moses and Aaron rightly pointed out that the "grumblings are not against us but against the LORD" (Ex. 16:8). The blaming is actually blasphemy against God.

Grumbling focuses on the brown grass and masks the core of the complaint that is leveled at God Himself, who is the very means of grace. In Israel's case, memory distorted the mercy of deliverance from Egypt into misery in the desert. The Israelites diminished God's grace to such a smallness that it disappeared like a mirage in the wilderness of sin and turned a mercy into a murmuring.[3] From the midst of the murmuring, God graciously provided quail and also manna that rained down from heaven "that He might make you understand that man does not live by bread alone, but man lives by everything that proceeds out of the mouth of the LORD" (Deut. 8:3).

In His divine wisdom, God planned to use manna not only to teach the Israelites in the wilderness but later to teach a grander lesson through Christ. In John 6, Jesus fed the five thousand; and the people found Him the next day on the other side of the sea. Christ quickly exposed their motives; they sought Him because their stomachs were filled (John 6:26). The crowd then asked, "What then do You do for a sign, so that we may see, and believe You? What work do You perform? Our fathers ate manna in the wilderness; as it is written, 'He gave them bread out of heaven to eat (John 6:30–31).'" The crowd credited the provision of manna to Moses and not God so that Jesus corrected and rightly proclaimed, "I am the bread of life; he who comes to Me will not hunger, and he who believes in Me will never thirst" (John 6:35). The crowd then grumbled (John 6:41).

Israel grumbled about the manna in the wilderness and now grumbled about the true manna, Jesus Christ the Bread of Life. The crowds failed to remember the first provision accurately as they misattributed the source of manna to Moses and then failed to recognize God's provision of the true, eternal manna in Christ. The cudgel of corrupted memory misguides from the provider of all good things and misleads to think the provision is not good enough.

3 Ibid. p. 90.

Nostalgia
••••••••••••••

Nostalgia also emerges from distortion of a good past. Grumbling and nostalgia intermingle. Again, Israel stumbled in their wilderness wanderings. Moses revealed that the "rabble who were among them had greedy desires" and incited Israel to cry out for meat (Num. 11:4). In their weeping, Israel said, "We remember the fish which we used to eat free in Egypt, the cucumbers and the melons and the leeks and the onions and the garlic, but now our appetite is gone. There is nothing at all to look at except this manna" (Num. 11: 5–6). God's provision of manna failed to satisfy, and now grumbling mingled with nostalgia rose up to God's ears. The people remembered Egypt with an exaggeration of the goodness of the past: slavery was distorted to freedom as they "ate freely" while in bondage.

The nostalgic Israelites selectively remembered past benefits while forgetting the context of slavery. While nostalgic, your affections travel back into the past instead of forward into future hope. Israel longed for the melons of slavery instead of pressing forward in hope of the grapes of the Promised Land. "Nostalgia hijacks memory. . . . In nostalgia, one sacrifices the present and the possibility of the future as one squats in the past. Nostalgia implies that God is present in one moment and not another, or more perniciously, that one prefers to be in a previous, unlivable moment more than the one God has brought them to now."[4]

Is your "good" past robbing your present joy? Heed the wise warning of Solomon who writes, "Do not say, 'Why is it that the former days are better than these?' For it is not from wisdom that you ask about this'" (Eccl. 7:10). Your good past may serve as a source for joy in the present but also may turn into a source of discontentment.

4 Kyle David Bennett, "Abandon all hope ye who forget," Web. 24 August, 2020, cardus.ca., 1 December, 2015.

DISTORTIONS OF A BAD PAST

Bitterness

···············

The cudgel of memory delivers blows with a "good" past, but what about a "bad" past? A distorted memory recalls the "bad" past to poison the present. To begin, bitterness mines the past with constant repetitive recitation of the wrongs and a forgetfulness of any blessings. Bitterness burns bridges and builds barriers. Bitterness may result from past sin but also may result from suffering, like in the case of Naomi.

The book of Ruth begins with Naomi, her husband, and two sons who left Bethlehem for Moab to escape famine (Ruth 1:1–2). During the time in Moab, Naomi's husband died (Ruth 1:3). Over the next ten years, her two sons married but then also both died (Ruth 1:5). At the height of Naomi's personal famine, bread returned to Bethlehem, "the house of bread." Naomi returned with her faithful daughter-in-law, Ruth. On her return to Bethlehem, Naomi told the women of the town, "Do not call me Naomi; call me Mara, for the Almighty has dealt very bitterly with me. I went out full, but the LORD has brought me back empty. Why do you call me Naomi [which means "pleasant"], since the LORD has witnessed against me and the Almighty has afflicted me?" (Ruth 1:20–21). Naomi's bitterness defined her life, even to provoke a name change, from pleasant to bitter. In examining her bitterness, Naomi identified God and His sovereignty as the source. She mangled the character of God, focusing on His sovereignty at the expense of His goodness and wisdom. Bitterness blinded Naomi to the blessing of Ruth. Naomi believed that she returned empty-handed when God filled her hands with Ruth.

In a way similar to your tongue that contains many more bitter than sweet taste receptors[5], your mind detects and fixates on bitterness at an alarmingly high rate and ignores the sweetness all around. However, unlike the tongue that uses bitterness to protect from poisons by inducing vomit, the bitterness of the mind produces a perverse savoring.

---

5 Danielle R. Reed et al, "Diverse tastes: Genetics of sweet and bitter perception." *Physiology & behavior* vol. 88,3 (2006): 215–26.

Regret

Regret also rewinds and replays. Regret bogs down the present with what could have been in the past. You resign yourself to the wretched conditions of the present like the prodigal son (Luke 15:16). Corrupted memory entraps you in the pigpen prison, and you keep lifting the slop to your mouth while squatting in the squalor of the past. Bitterness focuses on what has been done to you while regret targets what you have done to yourself. Memory mutters, "I wish things had gone differently," and, "If I just ...." The pronoun "I" dominates the recycled loop of thinking. American pastor and author, A. W. Tozer, agrees: "Regret may be no more than a form of self-love. A man may have such a high regard for himself that any failure to live up to his own image of himself disappoints him deeply. This state of mind crystallizes finally into a feeling of chronic regret which appears to be a proof of deep penitence but is actually proof of deep self-love."[6] This deception roots in the belief that you possess the strength and ability to have directed your steps differently to have achieved the desired and better outcome.

Ironically, regret can be birthed out of maturity, the older self assessing the younger self. The older man, though, fails to acknowledge that his present maturity grew out of his past failings that he now regrets. The older man forgets the surrounding context of the decision. The cudgel of corrupted memory bludgeons over and over.

Shame and Guilt

In other painful effects of corrupted memory, shame emphasizes the condemnation by others due to a perceived shortcoming from something done by you or done to you. Thus, shame associates with reputation as it is based on others' opinion of you. Shame claims to be unforgivable as it is not born out of a wrong act but rather something that is wrong with the entire person and a flawed identity. An apology falls short. Others disgrace you for these perceived shortcomings that may be sinful or may not (e.g.,

6 A. W. Tozer, "The futility of regret," *Alliance Life Magazine* published a compilation of essays in the book *That Incredible Christian* (Wingspread, 2008).

suffering). For instance, Jeremiah clearly states in an analogy a "thief is shamed when he is discovered." Publicized sin produces shame. However, shame also extends to suffering like David's servants who had their beards shaved off by Hunan and were greatly shamed (2 Sam. 10:4–5) but had not sinned. Whether associated with sin or suffering, shame eats away at your identity with feelings of worthlessness and whispers that you are marred, unworthy, and a mistake.

Today, shame and guilt are often used synonymously, but they are different from each other. Unlike shame, which is fear of worthlessness, guilt is fear of punishment. As such, "Guilt lives in the courtroom. Shame lives in the community."[7] Guilt arises internally from conviction and conscience, while shame arises externally from others' condemnations. In essence, shame emphasizes the loss of face before others, while guilt results from a loss of face before God. "Shame today is what lines up our actions horizontally. Guilt is what lines them up vertically."[8]

Guilt itself is not a sin and is utilized by God to turn a sinner to seek forgiveness. True guilt is conviction by the Holy Spirit due to known personal violation of God's law. The defective memory responds to guilt by running from repentance and wallowing. Wallowing carries the idea of rolling around in the mud and not seeking a way out, a vicious corruption of memory. Corrupted memory infects the soul with the problem and deprives of any solution.

The psalmist describes the torture of guilt without repentance as his "body wasting away" and his energy drained "as with the fever heat of summer" (Ps. 32:3–4). To avoid confession, unrepentant guilt might meander into the slippery solution of self-forgiveness. In this distortion, memory recalls to mind the wrongs of the past, and then directs to self for the solution. Like Adam and Eve, the guilty sew together their own solution to make amends with fig leaf coverings when they actually need the covering sacrifice that only comes from the Savior (Gen. 3:7). Self-forgiveness elevates man's solution above God's. Man attempts to be his own lenient judge, even

---

7 Edward T. Welch, *Shame Interrupted* (New Growth Press, 2012), 11.

8 David Wells, *The Courage to be Protestant*. 2nd Ed. (Eerdmans, 2017), 132.

though he is not the offended party. The fundamental flaw of self-forgiveness then resides in a corrupted self remembrance, the magnification of self-righteousness and minimization of offense. Self-forgiveness is no forgiveness at all. The offense remains like a garbage bag full of rotting fish that gets moved from sitting on the kitchen floor to out of sight under the sink. Out of sight is not out of mind, as your nose will detect soon enough. Unrepentant sin worsens over time.

Sin is like the seeds of a Pisonia tree. These seeds entrap insects with a sticky resin.[9] The sticky seeds laden with insects lure birds with the hope of a tasty feast. As the birds snack on lunch, they are snagged by lunch. The seed resin sticks to bird feathers. As the birds accumulate these seeds on their feathers, they are eventually weighed down and unable to fly as they cannot remove these seeds on their own. Covered in sticky Pisonia seeds, the birds die either on the tropical forest floor or suspended from the sticky tree. Unrepentant sin sticks like these seeds. Memory prompts guilt, a sense of the burden over sin; and yet corrupted memory wallows or excuses itself in self-forgiveness. Meanwhile, the seeds are still attached—the guilty condition remains. In truth, "You do not need to supplement divine forgiveness with any self-forgiveness,"[10] but man continues to run the opposite direction away from God, burdened and weighed down by his unrepentant sin.

The corrupt memory constantly gravitates away from God and toward self. The memory cudgel claims to be a scepter, picked up by man to claim his own self-rule and sit on his own throne. However, the memory cudgel serves you wrongly by beating you away from the throne room of God. Fallen memory desires to serve self and yet it damages self. The common phrase "If my memory serves me well," emphasizes this fundamental problem; when memory serves me, things never go well.

9 Alan E. Burger, "Dispersal and Germination of Seeds of Pisonia Grandis, an Indo-Pacific Tropical Tree Associated with Insular Seabird Colonies," *Journal of Tropical Ecology*, vol. 21, no. 3 (2005), 263–71.

10 H. B. Charles, "How can I forgive myself?", Web. 24 August, 2020, ftc.co, 24 August 2017.

Chapter 3
Application Questions

1. What are some recent circumstances when you grumbled? Did your grumbling involve comparisons in any way?

2. What is the difference between the sin of nostalgia and the delight of a past memory?

3. Do you have any bitterness from the past? Has bitterness benefited you in any way? What is holding you back from putting bitterness to death?

4. What is your biggest regret in life? What emotions do you associate with regret?

5. What are the similarities and differences between shame and guilt? When was the last time you experienced shame or guilt?

4

God's Remedy for Memory

In my childhood backyard, my mind travels from the treehouse and down the steep hill back toward the house until I stop right next to my parent's bedroom window, the place I almost died. When I was five years old, a water truck parked in the lot behind my house rolled down this same hill and crashed through the fence into my parents' bedroom window and closet. Clothes and pink insulation covered the ground. My parents panicked. At the time, we were all playing in the backyard, but I had been standing in the place the truck now stood. The ground no longer shows the ruts of the tire tracks, but the ruts in my memory remain.

In a similar way, the corrupt pervasiveness of memory creates a sense of helplessness like a truck that barrels down a hill at a child on a path of imminent destruction. No one is able to escape the sin that distorts the mind away from God through self-serving ways and with self-harming effects. "All of us have sinned and fall short of the glory of God" (see Rom. 3:23), and "each of us has turned to his own way" (Isa. 53:6a). Sin is universal, including the sin of the mind. Sin would be inconsequential if it were hidden from the judge, but God sees all and calls your sin to account (Jer. 14:10). Hosea warns, "He will remember their iniquity, He will punish their sins" (Hos. 9:9b). God's perfect memory of iniquity perpetuates His justice. In the fullness of His attributes, God does not suppress His justice as His justice must be fully expressed. The judge declares the penalty for sin is death (Rom. 6:23a). Death is inevitable and deserved.

The story of mankind does not end in hopelessness, as the verse continues: "but the free gift of God is eternal life in Christ Jesus our Lord" (Rom. 6:23b). How is this possible? Isaiah 53:6b finishes, "but the Lord has caused the iniquity of us all to fall on Him." These verses contrast the deserved sinful state of man with the undeserved grace of God's plan. God interjected into time and space; His Son broke the spiral of hopeless condemnation to provide a way of redemption.

THE PERFECT MEMORY OF THE REDEEMER

His perfect memory of Scripture

The Son of God took on human flesh and dwelt among men (John 1:14; Rom. 8:3). The incarnation remains unfathomable and yet a known historical reality. Jesus, born to the virgin Mary (Gal. 4:4), was fully man and yet remained fully God. Christ's humanity did not dilute His divinity (Phil. 2:7–8). "For in Him all the fullness of Deity dwells in bodily form" (Col. 2:9) Irenaeus, an early church father, observed that He "became what we are so that He might make us what He is."[1] For Christ's righteousness to be credited to guilty sinners, Christ lived a perfect life without any sin (1 Peter 2:22).

In living a perfect life, Christ exemplified an unblemished memory. Following the start of His public ministry, Jesus was tempted in the wilderness by Satan (Matt. 4:1). After Jesus fasted for forty days, Satan questioned the Father's provision for His Son. Christ passed the test with remembering "that man does not live by bread alone, but man lives by everything that proceeds out of the mouth of the LORD" (Deut. 8:3). In Deuteronomy 8:2, God commanded Israel to "remember all the ways which the LORD your God led." Christ did remember the Scripture and conquered, where Israel forgot and failed. Unlike the first Adam who ate the forbidden fruit in the ideal conditions of the garden, Jesus,

---

1 Irenaeus. *Against Heresies.* Book 5, preface.

the second Adam, didn't create and eat bread for Himself in the wilderness.

In the second temptation, Satan quoted God's words but out of context and with improper application. He commanded Christ to throw Himself off the pinnacle of the temple. Quoting Psalm 91:11–12, the tempter conveniently did not continue on, "You will tread upon the lion and cobra, the young lion, and the serpent you will trample down. Because he has loved Me, I will set him securely on high, because he has known My name. He will call upon Me, and I will answer Him; I will be with him in trouble; I will rescue him and honor him. With a long life I will satisfy him and let him see My salvation" (Ps. 91:13–16). Jesus stood on the pinnacle of the temple next to the tempter with intimate knowledge of His Father's love that set him on high to trample the serpent and fulfill prophecy from the garden of Eden! In response to Satan, Jesus perfectly recalled and applied Scripture, "You shall not put the LORD your God to the test" (Deut. 6:16).

Finally, Satan presented the most sinister of temptations when he asked Christ to bypass God's plan. "All these things I will give You if You fall down and worship me" (Matt. 4:9). In a display of authority, Jesus ordered Satan to leave, and quoted Scripture: "You shall worship the LORD your God, and serve Him only" (Deut. 6:13). Christ had perfectly followed the prior verse to "watch yourself that you do not forget the LORD" (Deut. 6:12a). Satan attacked God's provision, power, and plan, but Christ faced temptation and remembered Scripture, the very Scriptures that contained commands to remember. He remembered, where Israel failed and forgot.

His perfect memory in prayer

Christ demonstrated perfect memory not only through words of Scripture but also in words of prayer. Prayer is an act of remembrance. Christ perfectly exemplified prayer to His people at all times of the day and night. Jesus prayed "in the early morning while it was still dark" (Mark 1:35) and in evening spending "the whole night in prayer to God" (Luke 6:12). Jesus patterned prayer in everyday events like blessing the food (Matt. 14:19; Mark 8:6; Luke 24:30) but also prayed in major events.

Prayer permeated every major milestone in His ministry. His public ministry began with prayer at His baptism. "[A]nd while He was praying, heaven was opened" (Luke 3:21). Christ also prayed all night and then chose the twelve disciples, including Judas (Luke 6:12–13). Luke recorded that Jesus took Peter, James, and John up the mountain, "and while He was praying, the appearance of His face became different, and His clothing became white and gleaming" (Luke 9:28–29). Prayer marked the final day that led up to the cross with the last supper (Luke 22:19) and high-priestly prayer (John 17) and culminated with the pleading in the garden. Unlike the first Adam who failed and fled, the second Adam fell on His knees and faced the cross. The first Adam disobeyed the command to not eat the fruit of the one tree; the second Adam now drank the cup poured out on the tree. Christ's divine obedience rested in his divine remembrance of the will of His loving Father.

Christ's prayers did not just precede the cross but continued on the cross. Christ prayed Scripture as He pleaded for the forgiveness of His crucifiers "for they do not know what they do" (Ps. 22:18). He cried out again, "My God, my God, why have You forsaken me (Ps. 22:1)?" Finally, his last words quoted and fulfilled Psalm 31:5, "Father, into Your hands I commit My Spirit." Christ's memory perfectly called to mind in prayer the Word of God with His final words to His Father. Prayer marked the start of Jesus' public ministry in baptism and the end at the cross. "In the days of His flesh, He offered up both prayers and supplications with loud crying and tears to the One able to save Him from death, and He was heard because of His piety" (Heb. 5:7). Jesus Christ manifested perfect memory as He lived a perfect life, and "having been made perfect, He became to all those who obey Him the source of eternal salvation" (Heb. 5:8).

THE PERFECT PLAN OF REDEMPTION

The Pattern
· · · · · · · · · · · · · · · · ·

Christ Himself helps you better understand this perfect redemption through His conversation with Nicodemus about new birth and eternal life (John 3). Jesus provided a pattern for all of redemption including memory: the good original design, man's corruption of the good, and God's restoration to an even better state.

The imagery Christ uses with Nicodemus goes back to the wanderings of Israel in the desert. The people of Israel complained about the provision of "miserable food," manna (Num. 21:5). "The Lord sent fiery serpents among the people, and they bit the people "so that many died" (Num. 21:6). Grumbling, a sin of memory, led to death. The people cried out, "We have sinned" and asked Moses to "intercede with the LORD" (Num. 21:7). God instructed Moses to craft a bronze serpent and place it on a standard so that "everyone who is bitten, when he looks at it, will live" (Num. 21:8). God chose not to remove the serpents but to make a way of salvation through an intercessor. The bronze serpent should have served as a reminder of redemption, but eventually Israel turned it into an idol called Nehushtan (2 Kings 18:4). The image that God used for physical healing now led to spiritual illness; the symbol of God's mercy now spurred further judgment.

It would not be for another roughly 1,600 years until Christ redeemed the image with these words to Nicodemus, "As Moses lifted up the serpent in the wilderness, so must the Son of Man be lifted up, that whoever believes in Him may have eternal life" (John 3:14–15). Christ redeemed the image to a better state than the original. The original bronze serpent restored physical life for Israelites who believed, while Christ provides eternal life for all who believe! In His wisdom, God created a means of salvation through the better bronze serpent, Christ, to redeem His people to an even better state.

This divine pattern rings true for all creation, including human memory. Remember, the beautiful tree that represented the original created human memory broke with the weight of the curse with branches lying on the ground. These branches of memory serve as cudgels that you use to beat yourself away from God. The cross redeems the cudgel of corrupted memory. Christ who hung on the tree redeems the corrupted tree of memory and draws you close to God.

In Central American forests, a tree called the Chechem tree grows. Its bark and leaves contain an oily substance called urushiol, a chemical also found in poison ivy.[2] A blistering severe rash erupts when the oils touch your skin. Amazingly, the antidote grows close by in the form of the Chaka tree. Several bioactive components in the bark and leaves work together to shut down the body's inflammatory reaction to the oils. The trees, Chechem and Chaka, can grow right next to each other (less than 3 feet apart) and look very similar. To make the antidote, you take some Chaka leaves and boil them in a pot until the water is thick and crimson; and then apply it to heal the painful rash. In this sinful world, you walk through a forest with the oils of the Chechem tree sticking to you. God brings you to a place of utter helplessness, crying out that you have sinned and need a Savior. Standing right next to the harmful Chechem tree, Christ, like the Chaka tree, stands. Christ died; and through His crimson blood, your sins will be made white like wool (Isa. 1:18b).

The Accusation
....

At the cross, Jesus paid the debt of sin for you that you could not pay. Paul writes, "When you were dead in your transgressions and the uncircumcision of your flesh, He made you alive together with Him, having forgiven us all our transgressions, having canceled out the certificate of debt" and "nailed it to the cross" (Col. 2:13–14). For God's justice to be fully satisfied (as God remembers every single sin), every single sin must be accounted for and nailed to the cross. Satan brings accusations to God regarding His people and leverages the law against the lawbreakers.

Satan reminds God of His people's failures and unworthiness. These accusations appeal to God's holiness and justice against His people. However, those who believe in Him say, "If God is for us, who is against us? He who did not spare His own Son, but delivered

2 John Peck, "The incredible coincidence of a poisonous tree growing next to its antidote," Web. 24 August, 2020, atlasobscura.com, 6 June, 2016.

Him over for us all, how will He not also with Him freely give us all things? Who will bring a charge against God's elect? God is the one who justifies; who is the one who condemns? Christ Jesus is He who died, yes, rather who was raised, who is at the right hand of God, who also intercedes for us" (Rom. 8:31–34). The pardon for sin paid the full price as God remembered every single sin and nailed every one to the cross for you, His child. If only one sin was unknown and forgotten, God's justice would be imperfect; Satan would have grounds for accusation. What a terrifying thought to stand in judgment with unpaid-for sin! Yet, we take comfort that the accuser, "who accuses [us] before our God day and night" (Rev. 12:10) is conquered so that nothing will separate us from the love of God, which is in Christ Jesus our Lord (Rom. 8:39). Praise the Lord that "my sin, not in part, but the whole is nailed to the cross."[3]

The Transaction

However, a mysterious transaction of memory takes place at the cross. God not only remembers every single sin in His perfect justice, but He also forgets every sin in His perfect mercy. The psalmist poetically rejoices, "He has not dealt with us according to our sins, nor rewarded us according to our iniquities. For as high as the heavens are above the earth, so great is His loving-kindness toward those who fear Him. As far as the east is from the west, So far has He removed our transgressions from us" (Ps. 103:10–12). Isaiah reiterates, "I am the one who wipes out your transgressions for My own sake, and I will not remember your sins" (Isa. 43:25).

How is this possible for God to forget sin when He possesses perfect memory? Would this undermine His perfect character? Spurgeon exclaims, "The Lord cannot in strict accuracy of speech forget anything: forgetfulness is an infirmity, and God has no infirmities." He clarifies, "The Lord does not exercise memory as you and I do. We recall the past, but He has no past: all things are present with Him."[4] God, though, chose to use human terms

3 Horatio Gates Spafford, *When Peace, Like a River*, https://hymnary.org/text/when_peace_like_a_river_attendeth_my_way

4 Charles H. Spurgeon, "God's non-remembrance of sin," 22 October, 1881, Web. 24 August, 2020, spurgeon.org.

like memory and forgetfulness because "He wishes us to know that His pardon is so true and deep that it amounts to an absolute oblivion, a total forgetting of all the wrong-doing of the pardoned ones."[5]

Forgetfulness expresses the depth and completeness of the pardon for sin. Forgetfulness also implies that God's "infinite mind is not revolving within itself the tale of our iniquities."[6] To clarify, forgetfulness does not mean "to make sin not to have been or not to have been sin but not to be punished as it deserves."[7] In a judicial sense, then, as Judge, God does not take action against us and decree deserved punishment. He forgives and wipes the offense off the record.

How is divine forgetfulness accomplished such that "I will forgive their iniquity, and their sin I will remember no more" (Jer. 31:34; Heb. 10:17)? The author of Hebrews rightly argues that the better covenant was ushered in by the perfect high priest, Jesus, who offered one sacrifice once and for all (Heb. 10:12). The perfect sacrifice at the cross by our great High Priest secured divine forgetfulness, perfect pardon.

Therefore, the cross sits at the center of an amazing transaction of God's remembrance in justice and God's forgetfulness in mercy. His justice is satisfied in punishment while His mercy is satisfied in pardon.[8] The transaction at the cross is God's "masterpiece, wherein He means to bring all His attributes upon the stage."[9] The psalmist expresses this cataclysmic collision where "lovingkindness and truth have met together; righteousness and peace have kissed each other. Truth springs from the earth and righteousness looks down from heaven" (Ps. 85:10–11). The cross planted on earth in time extends its reach east and west while springing up from the earth to connect humanity and deity.

---

5 Ibid.

6 Ibid.

7 Matthew Henry, "Concise Commentary on Isaiah 38," *Matthew Henry Concise Commentary on the Whole Bible,* Web. 10 September, 2020, studylight.org.

8 Stephen Charnock, *Discourses upon the Existence and Attributes of God* (London: Thomas Tegg, 1840), 360.

9 Thomas Goodwin, *Christ the Mediator,* in *The Works of Thomas Goodwin,* D.D., ed. Thomas Smith (1861–1866); (reprint, Grand Rapids: Reformation Heritage Books, 2006), 5:16.

To secure the pardon for all who believe, Christ suffered the forgetfulness of the Father on the cross. At the culmination, Christ cried out, "My God, my God, why have You forsaken Me?" To be forsaken by the Father expresses the deepest sense of forgetfulness that anyone can experience. Christ was forsaken so that those who believe will never be forsaken by God. In light of Christ's forsakenness at the cross, God will never forsake you (Heb. 13:5) as that would be, in essence, forsaking Himself and rejecting His own Son's sacrifice. Spurgeon reiterates that forgetting "means that God will never seek any further atonement."[10] "Once and for all, the eternal consequences were removed; and God will not again rule as Judge and retry the case."[11] Forgiveness is fixed and final. God forgets.

The Resurrection

How do you know that the sacrifice by Christ was sufficient once and for all? Because the Son did not remain forsaken by the Father. In the ultimate display of satisfaction by the sacrifice of the Son, God raised Jesus from the dead "putting an end to the agony of death" (Acts 2:24). Resurrection is remembrance. To the very depths that Christ was forsaken at the cross, His resurrection represents the very pinnacle of remembrance in all of human history.

The resurrection is of first importance and a necessity to the gospel. The cross without the empty tomb leaves your faith empty (1 Cor. 15:17). The transaction of memory must be completed or else the debt of sin remains. All my sin is remembered and nailed to the cross in God's justice; and yet, all my sin is forgotten and removed by God's mercy. The Son of God was forsaken on the cross to pardon sin; but God remembered His Son in His resurrection and glorification. The mystery of this memory transaction exceeds human comprehension. Only God's plan stretches to these depths of payment and heights of pardon.

In light of this precious and costly pardon, God offers freely the gift of grace to all who believe. "For by grace you have been saved through faith; and that not of yourselves, it is the gift of

10 Charles H. Spurgeon, "God's non-remembrance of sin," 22 October 1881, Web. 24 August, 2020. spurgeon.org.

11 Ibid.

God; not as a result of works, so that no one may boast" (Eph. 2:8–9). Salvation reorients boasting back toward God and away from self, as you did not do anything to deserve this gift of grace. How should you respond? Believe (Acts 16:31) and repent (Rom. 10:9) as you remember the cross and the grave.

Glorification

Christ's work continues in His glorification. Christ ascended to the throne, but His work continues in divine intercession, a continual remembrance of His people. The writer of Hebrews says that Christ holds His priesthood permanently and forever. "Therefore He is able also to save forever those who draw near to God through Him, since He always lives to make intercession for them" (Heb. 7:25). Christ's permanency provides eternal security for all who believe. Christ, who laid down His life as the sacrifice on the altar, now intercedes as the High Priest.

As a believer, recount these truths over and over. The old, old story will truly never grow old; and its retelling will never leave you disappointed. You will be able to look back like Christian in *The Pilgrim's Progress* and remember the day you ran up Calvary's hill with the burden of sin on your back to then come to the foot of the cross.[12] The burden loosened, fell from his shoulders, and rolled down the hill into the mouth of the grave below. Freedom!

THE COVENANT APPLICATION OF PERFECT REDEMPTION

God remembers His covenant

Because of Christ's work on the cross, God has remembered and fulfilled His covenants, just as He promised. Covenant requires remembrance. The cross reaches back in remembrance to the first covenant with Adam where the promise was fulfilled that Christ would crush the head of the serpent (Gen. 3:15). The Bible consistently reverberates back to the garden to demonstrate God's perfect plan to redeem sinful man from the fall.

12 John Bunyan, *The Pilgrim's Progress* (London: Gall and Inglis, undated), 49.

With Noah

·················

Following the flood, God makes a covenant with Noah. In the flood, God "blotted out every living thing that was upon the land" (Gen. 7:23), "but God remembered Noah" (Gen. 8:1) and all the animals in the ark, and rescued them. This is the first time the word "remember" or "*dakar*" appears in the Bible. Imagine the importance of God's remembrance to Noah who listened to the waters prevail for 150 days until he finally heard "a wind pass over the earth" and dry land appeared just like in the original creation account. After God remembered and rescued Noah, He established a covenant of remembrance to never send a flood to destroy the earth again and set the rainbow in the sky as a reminder to man of His covenant (Gen. 9:11–13).

With Abraham

·····················

God instituted a covenant with Abraham to make him a great nation and to bless all the nations of the earth (Gen. 12:1–3). God remembered His covenant to Abraham through the establishment of the nation of Israel through Isaac and Jacob. As the nation of Israel multiplied while in Egyptian bondage, a pivotal moment transpired: Israel cried out to God. "So God heard their groaning; and God remembered His covenant with Abraham, Isaac, and Jacob." Covenant remembrance and redemption intertwine (Ps. 111:9).

With Moses

·················

God redeemed His people out of slavery and led them to Mount Sinai where Moses received the law of the covenant. In the Mosaic covenant, God gave the people conditions with blessings for obedience and consequences for disobedience. Despite these warnings, Israel failed. Despite Israel forgetting God, He promised not to forget them because He "is a compassionate God; He will not fail you nor destroy you" (Deut. 4:31). God remembers His covenant out of self-remembrance. God swears upon Himself (Isa. 45:23). His perfect covenant-keeping memory rests upon His perfect character.

With David

•••••••••••••••

In the same manner, God entered into a covenant with King David to "establish the throne of his kingdom forever" (2 Sam. 7:13). Again, David failed; but God promised His "lovingkindness shall not depart from him" (2 Sam. 7:15). David's failings are well known, and the Davidic kingly line trended downward to the low point of the Babylonian captivity; but God kept His covenant in His lovingkindness and sent Jesus, the Son of David, to save the House of David.

With the New Covenant

••••••••••••••••••••••••••••

The son of David, Jesus Christ, ushered in the new covenant. Mary exalted the Lord for blessing her as she learned that she was to be the mother of the Messiah. She worshiped God who "has given help to Israel His servant, in remembrance of His mercy, as He spoke to our fathers, to Abraham and his descendants forever" (Luke 1:55). Mary worshiped as she recognized that God in His mercy remembered His covenant through Jesus. Zacharias, John the Baptist's father, blessed the Lord for redemption of His people "to show mercy toward our fathers, and remember His holy covenant, the oath which He swore to Abraham our father" (Luke 1:72–72). The Messiah represented redemptive remembrance wrapped in mercy. The Sunrise of the Savior reminded the people that God had not forgotten His promises (Luke 1:78).

Christ not only fulfilled prior covenants but mediated a better new covenant. This new covenant redeemed His people who believed before the cross and redeemed His people who believed after the cross (Heb. 10:15). His covenantal remembrance transcends time because God is not bound by the time He created. The sacrifice of Christ eclipses space as the sacrifice is made available to anyone who believes across all borders and ethnic divides. Thus, His boundless memory coupled with His boundless mercy keeps His covenants to His people. "For all the promises of God find their Yes in Him. That is why it is through Him that we utter our Amen to God for his glory" (2 Cor. 1:20).

THE PERSONAL APPLICATION OF PERFECT REDEMPTION

God remembers the needy

••••••••••••••••••••••••••••••

God remembers His covenants that apply collectively to His people as a whole, but does the God of the universe remember people individually? The Bible answers: Yes! Not only does God remember His people but especially notices and helps the needy and afflicted. David reflected this truth when he said, "For the needy will not always be forgotten, nor the hope of the afflicted perish forever" (Ps. 9:18). David illustrated: "You have taken account of my wanderings; put my tears in Your bottle. Are they not in Your book?" (Ps. 56:8). God uses your tears from His bottle to write a grand story that far surpasses your feeble comprehension. In the darkest of times, the salty transparent tears of the saints transform into a black permanent ink, etched onto the mind of God.

Hannah, who had no children, was oppressed by her rival, Peninnah, who did have children. Her rival provoked her, constantly reminding Hannah of her childlessness. When Hannah went up to the temple in great distress, she prayed to the Lord and wept bitterly (1 Sam. 1:10). Hannah vowed, "O Lord of hosts, if You will indeed look on the affliction of Your maidservant and remember me, and not forget Your maidservant, but will give Your maidservant a son, then I will give him to the Lord all the days of his life, and a razor shall never come on his head" (1 Sam. 1:11). Soon after she returned from the temple to her home, "the Lord remembered her (1 Sam. 1:19)," and "she gave birth to a son, and she named him Samuel saying, 'Because I have asked him of the Lord'" (1 Sam. 1:20). Hannah's tears collected in God's bottle; and God wrote a book, a story better than Hannah could have ever hoped or imagined, with her son Samuel. Throughout the Bible, God shows that His eye sees and His ear hears the cries of the oppressed; and He acts.

God remembers His sheep
••••••••••••••••••••••••••••••••

Jesus alluded to this personal remembrance for His people as a shepherd. Jesus identified Himself as the Good Shepherd who knows His sheep by name, personally and specifically. Jesus not only called and led His sheep but voluntarily laid down His life for His sheep on His own initiative out of love. Jesus elevated the illustration as He is not only the Good Shepherd but also the Lamb.

As the Lamb of God hung on the cross, the religious leaders and two thieves hurled insults at Him, questioning His power to save and be saved (Matt. 23:42–44). Yet, darkness fell and one of the thieves began to see the darkness of his own heart. He rebuked the other thief and acknowledged that they were suffering justly for their evil deeds, but that Christ had done nothing wrong (Luke 23:40–41). Then, the thief asked the Lamb, "Jesus, remember me when you come in Your kingdom" (Luke 23:42). In the darkness that shrouded the cross, the light shone into the heart of this man as Christ proclaimed, "Truly I say to you, today, you shall be with Me in Paradise." The Good Shepherd led this brokenhearted sheep to rest in the meadows of heaven.

Just like the thief on the cross, we need to recognize our helpless state. Because of the curse of sin, each human being faces the darkness of eternal death, separation from God in hell. This disturbing reality may be suppressed by the deception that death is far off, a problem for a distant tomorrow. The Lord may provide reminders with near-death experiences like the truck that hurtled down the hill of my backyard at me. On that near fatal day, my recollection skips from the crashing sound of the fence to the fire truck sirens in the front of my house. At five years old, no one knows how I ended up jumping the side fence to safety. In His plan, God saved me that day from physical death; and then five years later saved me from spiritual destruction.

Chapter 4
Application Questions

1. How did Christ utilize His memory in the wilderness temptation? Why is context important in the application of Scripture memory?

2. What examples does Christ provide for the use of memory in prayer?

3. Describe, in your own words, the transaction of memory that took place at the death and resurrection of Jesus.

4. What response do you have to the account of the thief on the cross?

5. If you have had a near-death experience, how did this affect you?

5

Tools to Sanctify Memory

God not only remembers His sheep in salvation but also continues to remember His sheep in sanctification, the progressive spiritual growth of a believer in this life. Positionally, those who believe are new creatures in Christ (2 Cor. 5:17); sin no longer reigns with control over the mind and heart, blinding believers to the truth. Sin was conquered at the cross, but the battle rages on against the flesh in this world. Human memory battles with the remnants of indwelling sin. To reiterate, you forget what you should remember and remember what you should forget, while doubting that God will forget what He promised and will remember what He promised to forget.

At the moment of salvation, God does not bestow upon you a perfect memory as you still battle the flesh in a fallen world. In fact, God uses imperfect memory in the sanctifying process to drive you back to Him in humility and reliance. These failings of memory, like a deep thirst, lead the battle-weary back to the well of everlasting water.

In the process of sanctification, God does not leave His people empty-handed but assists them. The Puritan, Joseph Alleine, prayed, "Lord if you have given me Christ, will you now also with him provide everything I need?"[1] The answer is a resounding

1 Joseph Alleine, "Come in Your all-sufficiency," *Piercing Heaven: Prayers of the Puritans,* ed. Robert Elmer (Lexham Press, 2019), 109.

yes! God does not save what He then will not protect, preserve, and sanctify. God did not spill the precious and priceless blood of Christ to purchase a treasure that He neglects; rather He richly supplies all you need for life and godliness (2 Peter 1:3) through the surpassing greatness of His power and might, the same power that raised Christ from the dead (Eph. 1:18–20)! This power propels the believer forward into progressive transformation into the image of God (2 Cor. 3:18).

This step-by-step process on the path of sanctification is described as the light of dawn, that shines brighter and brighter until the full day" (Prov. 4:18). So, what means does God supply to help you transform your distorted memories? First and foremost, His Spirit!

THE INDWELLING OF THE HOLY SPIRIT

At the moment of salvation, the Holy Spirit indwells the believer and will be with the believer forever (John 14:16). When Jesus finished His earthly ministry, the Father sent the Spirit of truth. Jesus comforted the disciples and brought them such peace, saying that even though He was leaving, the Spirit was coming. God did not abandon His sheep but abides within them.

The Holy Spirit plays a vital role in sanctification and especially in memory of the truth. To provide assurance to His disciples, Jesus explained that "the Helper, the Holy Spirit, whom the Father will send in My name, He will teach you all things, and bring to your remembrance all that I said to you" (John 14:26). What a comfort that the Comforter would help the disciples rightly remember the truth.

The Father knows that the battle rages today, so He supplies His Spirit to transform your mind and redirect you to the truth. John Owen said that the Holy Spirit's work is "to bring the promises of Christ to our minds and hearts, to give us the comfort of them, the joy and sweetness of them."[2] The Holy Spirit's work in memory underpins all of the other aids God supplies for memory.

God, through the Holy Spirit, utilizes many tools to help His sheep remember rightly, like my dad's tools that filled the garage

2 John Owen, *The Works of John Owen*, ed. William H. Goold, vol. 2 (Johnstone & Hunter, 1850–1855; reprint, Edinburgh: Banner of Truth, 1965–1991), 237.

of my childhood home. On many Saturdays, my dad would be busy with a number of projects usually born out of necessity from a tight budget. My sisters and I would hover around, helping in small ways, grabbing tools to hand to him as he worked. The garage would serve as a wood shop to build new furniture pieces like beds, dressers, and tables. I enjoyed the assembly of new furniture, especially sanding and feeling the smoothed edges of the soft wood.

The garage also would convert into a mechanic's shop for car maintenance and car emergencies. Planned maintenance like an oil change kept the car running. In the garage, tools existed to make new things but also maintain and repair old things. Similarly, God uses many tools to make right memories and repair broken ones. Just as God supplied the wonderful gift of the Holy Spirit to indwell you, He also provides many tools not only all around you but also inside of you.

THE TOOL OF CONSCIENCE

The first tool to remember rightly dwells innately inside each human being—the conscience. The conscience is an awareness of right and wrong. Richard Sibbes, a Puritan theologian, commented that the conscience is a "conversation" of witness and testimony (Rom. 2:14–15) with "the soul reflecting upon itself."[3] Conscience functions in prevention and confession of sin. The conscience, like a pain for the soul, warns to prevent from sin and throbs when you do sin. The conscience, a gift from God, needs to be informed and calibrated to the perfect standard of God's Word. The Christian is called to give heed to the properly functioning conscience.

The fork-tailed Drogo is a bird that acts somewhat like a conscience. The Drogo keeps alert for predators like hawks and will chirp alarm calls to other animals.[4] A meerkat will pay attention to these calls and will run and hide to avoid predators like the hawk. The conscience is heeded, and danger is avoided.

3 Richard Sibbes, "An Exposition of 2 Corinthians Chapter 1," in *The Complete Works of Richard Sibbes*, ed. Alexander B. Grosart (1862–1864; reprint, Edinburgh: Banner of Truth Trust, 2001) 3: 208.

4 Jennifer Ackerman, *The Genius of Birds* (Penguin Books, 2017), 116.

However, the believer at times may wrongly choose to suppress and ignore true alarms of danger. If a true warning is given by the Drogo but goes unheeded by the meerkat, the hawk swoops down and captures the meerkat, the devastating outcome of a seared conscience (1 Tim. 4:2).

The conscience can also be improperly calibrated and misguide you into false sense of right and wrong. R. C. Sproul said the imperfect conscience "can speak out of both sides of its mouth, having capacity either to accuse or excuse."[5] The Drogo can also issue a false warning that danger is near. A meerkat will heed the call and drop a freshly caught meal to run and hide. The Drogo swoops down and will pick up the tasty meal while the meerkat stays hidden. A false alarm from a mis-calibrated conscience robs of the joy of forgiveness and inflicts with undue guilt.

To be properly employed, the conscience of a believer must be wielded by the Holy Spirit (Rom. 9:1) and guided by truth to serve the living God (Heb. 9:14). Praise the Lord for the help of the Spirit to give true warning of danger!

THE TOOL OF PRAYER

Prayer and the Holy Spirit are closely connected. Paul joins these together when he writes "the Spirit also helps our weaknesses; for we do not know how to pray as we should, but the Spirit Himself intercedes for us with groaning too deep for words; and He who searches the hearts knows what the mind of the Spirit is, because He intercedes for the saints according to the will of God" (Rom. 8:26–27). Prayer ascends from your lips, and the Spirit transforms these self-stained words into groaning intercessions in accordance with God's will.

Many times, prayer is the first step of a wayward wanderer back toward the path of right remembrance. This was the case for Christian and Hopeful, locked in Doubting Castle, beaten with the memory cudgel by Giant Despair for four days. To add to their misery, the giant showed them the bones and skulls of past pilgrims who dared to trespass on his land, whom he had torn

---

5 R. C. Sproul, *How Should I Live in this World?* (Reformation Trust Publishing, 2019), 110.

apart into pieces.[6] The giant brought them back to their dungeon hole, beating them on the way.

That Saturday night, the giant talked to his wife, Diffidence (meaning distrust), who advised him to search the pilgrims in the morning for any signs of hope for escape, like a picklock or key. The giant vowed to search them in the morning. Despair whispered in the prisoner's ears, "Is there a way out?" Diffidence questioned, "Is that even the right way?" At midnight, Christian and Hopeful "began to pray, and continued in prayer till almost break of day."[7] The fate of Pilgrim and Hopeful would turn on the hinge of prayer.

To orient

Prayer is an act of remembrance. You must first remember to pray. You must remember who God is and trust He listens and cares. You must remember who you are, dependent on Him. You must remember your requests and praises. You must remember to wait in expectation (Ps. 5:3). "Memories of the past and confidences concerning the future conducted the man of God to the mercy seat to plead for the needs of the present."[8] Jonah tried to run away from God and his task to bring the warning of judgment and call to repentance to the enemy city of Nineveh. Despite his efforts to run from God, God humbled him. Finally, Jonah cried out from the belly of a great fish and "remembered the LORD, and my prayer came to You, into Your holy temple" (Jonah 2:7). Prayer can happen in any place at any time prompted by memory.

To appeal

To go one step further, prayer is not just an act of remembrance by the one praying but is actually an appeal to God's remembrance. The Bible provides a template for how to pray both in light of God's "forgetfulness" and God's "remembrance."

The paradox of simultaneous remembrance and forgetfulness

6 John Bunyan, *The Pilgrim's Progress* (London: Gall and Inglis, undated), 153–54.

7 Ibid.

8 Charles H. Spurgeon, "Psalm 9," in *The Treasury of David*, vol. 1 (Thomas Nelson Publishers, 1984), 99.

in prayer percolates throughout the Psalms. David prayed in Psalm 25:6–7, "Remember, O LORD, Your compassion and Your lovingkindnesses, for they have been from of old. Do not remember the sins of my youth or my transgressions; according to Your lovingkindness remember me, for Your goodness' sake, O LORD." David pleaded with God for God to remember Himself, His own compassion and lovingkindness, while David's own corrupted memory had forgotten God when he sinned. Moreover, David then remembered his sin in confession and implored God to then forget his sin because of God's self-remembrance.

Notice, David uses the active imperative voice, calling God to remember and forget. David is not directing God in these prayers but rather leveraging God's own self-remembrance to accomplish God's promises. God is the subject of the prayer as He is the one to carry out this prayer, and He does. The prayer then appeals to God's self-remembrance, and His answer demonstrates He remembers.

To approach

Prayer inspires boldness when the believer remembers God. "This is the confidence which we have before Him, that, if we ask anything according to His will, He hears us. And if we know that He hears us in whatever we ask, we know that we have the requests which we have asked from Him" (1 John 5:14–15). How do we know that we pray in His will? Pray the promises of God. Spurgeon preached, "Prayer is the promise utilized. A prayer which is not based on a promise has no true foundation."[9] Prayer is the believer remembering to remind God to do what He promised.[10]

To outlast

In uttering a prayer in a moment of time, you ask God, who is not bounded by time, to remember in His good time. Your prayer outlasts you. Like a spark, the prayer rises up to God but like an ember it glows forever. Prayer spans generations and acknowledges

9 Charles H. Spurgeon, "The secret of power in prayer," 8 January 1888, Web. 24 August, 2020. spurgeon.org.

10 Ibid.

that God's answer is not confined to your own finite time on earth but rather expanded to God's boundless timing. Jesus prayed generationally when He asked not only for His disciples to be sanctified in truth but "for those also who believe in Me through their word." Jesus prayed for you over 2,000 years ago, and God remembers this prayer and accomplishes it today!

George Mueller prayed every day for the same five friends.[11] When he died over fifty-three years later, four of the five believed in Jesus. A couple months after his death, the final friend believed. George Mueller's persistent prayers ended at his final breath. Even though the prayer was no longer uttered on earth, it echoed in heaven.

Do not neglect to use this powerful tool of remembrance but also to record the answers. Keep a prayer journal to help you remember all the ways that God has answered and kept His promises to you. Remembrance of prayer is a panacea for the soul and brings perspective to past requests and praises. A prayer journal frees you to say with Charles Bridges that "no step well prayed over will bring ultimate regret."[12]

THE TOOL OF WRITTEN RECORDS

Written records are a common and ancient tool of remembrance. Only humans are able to read and transform strokes and dots into words that carry meaning and application. Writing and reading endow humans with an amazing tool to fight forgetfulness. "If not fixed upon paper, ideas are apt to vanish with the occasion which suggested them."[13] In fact, some see written records as a crutch and not a tool. Ironically, Plato wrote that writing would weaken memory as it would create reliance on what is written.[14] However, God created and clearly utilized the benefits of writing

11 John MacArthur, *The MacArthur New Testament Commentary: Matthew 16–23* (Moody Publishers, 2006), 81.

12 Charles Bridges, *A Commentary on Proverbs* (reprint, Edinburgh: The Banner of Truth Trust, 1998), 25.

13 Charles H. Spurgeon, *Feathers for Arrows: Illustrations for Preachers and Teachers* (London: Passmore and Alabaster, 1870), v.

14 Plato, *Phaedrus*, trans. W. C. Helmond and W. G. Rabinowitz (Indianapolis: Library of Liberal Arts, 1956), 68.

down His words; His words are not a crutch but a cure for the mind. Exodus 17 is the first place that God commands Moses to write down in "a book as a memorial" of the first military victory of Israel over an enemy, Amalek. The most famous Old Testament written record comes later in Exodus 14 when Moses wrote down the words of the Lord, the Law (Ex. 24:4).

Importance of written records

So important was a written law that God commanded each future king of Israel to write down his own copy of the law in the presence of a priest so that it would be with him. The written law directed the king's heart to "fear the LORD his God by carefully observing all these words" (Deut. 17:18–19).

Writing a record demonstrates importance—importance that the words not just be remembered for the present recipient but also for future generations. In Psalm 102, the faithfulness of God was written down "for the generation to come, that a people yet to be created may praise the LORD" (Ps. 102:18). Writing produces praise for God not just for the direct recipient but also for the future reader. The future reader benefits from the records of God's faithfulness to Abraham, Isaac, and Jacob; and praise to God does not just end with the death of the eyewitness but passes on to the present. Scribes preserved these treasures for today, like Hezekiah's men who transcribed Proverbs 25–29. Imagine ripping those five chapters out and losing forever the apples of gold in settings of silver (Prov. 25:11) or iron sharpening iron (Prov. 27:17). Ultimately, God used men like these to safeguard His words.

Transformation through written records

Entire generations may be transformed through written records as seen when Hilkiah the high priest found the book of the Law in the house of the Lord. When the book was brought and read to King Josiah, he tore his clothes and repented (2 Kings 22:8–13). The book was read to the entire nation, both small and great, with a response of repentance and reformation. Preserved words of God's law provoked a removal of evil priests, eradicating child sacrifice

(2 Kings 23:10) and culminated in the destruction of the idolatrous altar King Jeroboam had set up in Bethel. Fourteen prior kings tolerated and even worshiped at the altar of Jeroboam's golden calf "who brought you up out of the land of Egypt" (1 Kings 12:28), and it was destroyed by the reading of the lost law. Written words of God's Law incited the reformation of a nation and a return to worship.

On an even grander scale, the written words of the gospel awakened worldwide reformation that continues even to this day. The writers compiled these truths inspired by the Holy Spirit (2 Peter 1:19–21) to provide an eyewitness record to be handed down (Luke 1:1–2). As with prayer, the Holy Spirit actively brandishes the "sword of the Spirit, the word of God" (Eph. 6:17) to pierce our hearts and minds (Heb. 4:12). The words also may be sweet like honey (Ps. 19:10) and a salve for healing (Prov. 3:8). The Holy Spirit may convict or console with the same words. So do not neglect His Word preserved for you. Open the armory and the pharmacy for your soul.

Techniques in written records: Poetry

As a further aid to memory, writers employ different forms and techniques to grab the reader's attention and help the reader remember. Poetry enhances memory through the use of rhyme and rhythm. The rhyme and rhythm add richness to remembering. No longer are words locked on a blank white canvas; they are whirled in melodic color. God inspired biblical authors to write poetically to help His people remember His precious truths. Poets do not just use rhythm and rhyme but also will construct acrostics like rungs on a ladder, such as Psalm 119, which is composed of twenty-two stanzas that correspond with the twenty-two letters in the Hebrew alphabet.

Techniques in written records: Metaphors

Writers employ metaphors. Metaphors create pictures and associations that emblazon the writing from the page onto your mind and synchronize with the way you think. The human mind digests the world by learning with comparison of what you already know to what is new and lesser known.

These figures of speech add figure and shape to the invisible and abstract. For example, God describes Himself in metaphors to help you grapple with who He is. God is a rock, fortress, shepherd, strong tower, father, counselor, king, potter, physician, and bridegroom. Each of these metaphors for God emphasizes different aspects of God in vivid ways. God's tender care as a shepherd or His faithful discipline as a father moves you from easily overlooking to actually pondering. "Theology needs metaphor to capture aspects of reality that are easily caged."[15] Metaphors unlock these complexities.

Techniques in written records:
Parables and Storytelling

In a similar vein, parables and stories enhance and emphasize by drawing the reader in with the reader's own imagination. My dad was known for his stories. He based his stories on a character named Boswell and his sister Bertha. Boswell would go on mischievous adventures to teach lessons about honesty, kindness, and obedience. As I grew older, I realized these stories were entertaining but instructive, especially for me, because they were based on real-life events—my life. I was Boswell.

Turning to the Bible, the Gospel writers record the stories of the best storyteller of all time, Jesus. Rather than just tell the disciples that some will receive the gospel and bear fruit while others will reject it, Jesus tells of the Sower and the seed, a timeless parable that still holds the listener's attention today. Many of Jesus' parables point you to truth, and you identify with the story and its characters.

Techniques in written records: Repetition

To also add emphasis, writers use repetition; repetition repeats and stands in the road of the reader, waving its hands in the air to say, "Stop—stop and pay attention!" Christ used the phrase "truly, truly" to signal that something important was coming. Isaiah breaks the record for repetition in a single verse of the Bible

15 Jeffrey Arthurs, *Preaching as Reminding* (InterVarsity Press, 2017), 75.

when he writes, "Order on order, order on order, Line on line, line on line, A little here, a little there" (Isa. 28:10). The Great Hallel, Psalm 136, grabs and holds attention with repetition of the line, "For His lovingkindness is everlasting." The line repeats with a beat that carries His lovingkindness forward into eternity.

Writers use rhyme, rhythm, acrostics, metaphors, stories, and repetition to help the reader remember, and God employs these forms and techniques to further ingrain His word into your brain.

THE TOOL OF CREATION

God uses not only the writing on paper but also painting of creation to point to Himself. The earth is a roofless cathedral; the ceiling is painted in shifting hues of blues to deep violets, dotted with stars and the floor a mixture of lush greens and dusty browns, swirling with vibrant colors of the seasons. "The heavens are telling of the glory of God; and the expanse is declaring the work of His hands" (Ps. 19:1) so much so that men are without excuse as God has made Himself visible in His masterpiece (Rom. 1:20). You cannot miss Him, the artist clearly autographed His artwork so that He has been seen through what He has made.

Consider the wonders of God with Job (Job 37:14) and lift up your eyes on high and views the stars with Isaiah (Isa. 40:26). The same God created those same stars that you look at today, the same stars that God told Abraham to count. Abraham counted and believed God would fulfill His promise and reckon him righteous (Gen. 15:15). Reflect on the star that drew the magi from the East to worship the newborn King, and then let your mind dwell in worship on the star of Jacob (Num. 24:17), the bright morning star (Rev. 22:16), Jesus Christ. Creation leads you to worship the Maker of the stars and not to worship the stars themselves (Deut. 4:19; Amos 5:26–27). The cue of creation redirects to the primary purpose of memory, to worship and glorify the Lord.

To recognize smallness

Through the expanse of the heavens, God reminds man of his smallness. Man questions why God would be mindful and care for him in such a vast universe (Ps. 8:3). The self-awareness of smallness hits when you are flying high above a city in a plane and see all the tiny cars moving like ants along the streets or when you see a photo taken by the Hubble space telescope of 10,000 galaxies. The earth is indeed a "pale blue dot,"[16] and you are the dust on the dot. If you push your imagination beyond the firmament of stars, you will find that "it will soon exhaust the power of conception."[17] Your imagination cannot keep up with the vastness of the universe.

To recognize largeness

Reverse your imagination to then consider the smaller things of creation.[18] While sitting on a mount in the open air, Christ pointed to the birds of the air and reminded the disciples that the Father feeds and cares for them. Since there are an estimated 400 billion birds on planet Earth that all need food, water, and shelter, take comfort that you are worth more than these birds (Ps. 104:17; Matt. 6:26).[19] In this comparison, Christ established human dignity and value.

Let the large things of creation swallow up pride as you melt into the immensity of the Creator and forget self, but also let the small things in creation remind you of your immense value to God whose eye is on the sparrow (Matt. 10:31). Creation spawns self-forgetfulness and self-worth simultaneously. Humility and dignity do not compete but complement as they both find their origin in the Creator. Look up at the stars and see His greatness; and look to the birds of the air to see His care.

The blocking of creation's cues

16 Carl Sagan, *Pale Blue Dot* (Ballantine Books, 1997).

17 Blaise Pascal, "Of the means of belief," *Pensees,* 27 April, 2006, Web. 10 September, 2020, gutenberg.org.

18 Ibid.

19 K. J. Gaston and T. M. Blackburn, "How many birds are there?", *Biodiversity and Conservation* 6 (1997), 615–25.

So why is it difficult to remember God through creation? What hinders your worship of the Creator when the creation cues are all around you? First, science appeals to the distorted mind by the deception that explanation eliminates wonder. If humans can understand the earth around them and how it works, then science demotes and even explains away the Creator. If creation is more comprehensible, then maybe the Creator is comprehensible, explainable, and perhaps even unnecessary. And yet, miracles occur in creation every day (Prov. 30:18–19). Humans are no closer to making a single living cell than Adam was, but your body makes 2 million red blood cells per second.[20] Just because science can explain phototropism does not mean humans can create a flower that is able to bend and turn toward the light. Let the awe of phototropism bend your mind instead back to the true Light.

Worship in creation is also hindered by human achievement in the modernization of housing, heating and air conditioning, and media entertainment. All of these advances promote life indoors with minimal interaction with creation outdoors. In fact, average Americans spend 90 percent of their lifetime indoors.[21] These modern achievements may have many benefits, but be mindful of the potential hindrances they pose to creation's cues. Do not let the city lights dim out the lights of heaven and God's glory all around you. The roof and walls of your house provide protection from the heat and snow but also might mute the cues that point to the Maker. As you take shelter under your roof, the roof might block the view of a colorful rainbow, a sign in the sky placed for you to remember that God remembers (Gen. 9:15–16). Take shelter inside but don't forget to take a walk in search of reminders of God's promises.

Wonder at your worth as you watch the blue jay feed and ponder your smallness as you sit on the blue dot spinning suspended in space.

20 Billie Rubin, "How long do red blood cells live?", 31 December, 2010, Web. 11 September, 2020, *stanfordbloodcenter.org.*

21 U.S. Environmental Protection Agency. 1989. Report to Congress on indoor air quality: Volume 2. EPA/400/1-89/001C. Washington, DC.

Chapter 5
Application Questions

1. At salvation, your memory is not instantly perfected. Who helps you step-by-step in the transformation of memory? What tools are used?

2. What is a dulled or seared conscience? Why is this dangerous?

3. Do you ever use memory language in your prayers to God like David in Psalm 25:6–7? What would be some ways to incorporate memory into your prayer life?

4. Why are written records important for memory? Do you keep any written records to help your spiritual life?

5. How does creation balance smallness and largeness? Why is that balance important?

6

Cues to Sanctify Memory

God strategically employs the memory that He designed. God advantageously realigns your mind toward Him with declarative memory. Declarative memory, which includes memory for facts and meaning about the world, breaks down into two categories: semantic memory and episodic memory.

Semantic memory
....

Semantic memory covers long-term memory that helps you recall words, concepts, meanings, and numbers.[1] The vastness of this general knowledge for each individual may not be overestimated. You may walk up to any stranger on the street and start to test his memory and discover a vocabulary of up to 100,000 words, mastery of a second language, knowledge of facts about his country, credit card numbers, and the list would go on and on.

Episodic memory
....

Episodic memory involves memory of specific events[2] like a birthday party or a baseball game. Semantic memory recites

1 Alan Baddeley, *Essentials of Human Memory* (Psychology Press, 2014), 130.
2 Ibid., 16.

facts about the Atlantic Ocean and Cape May Beach, while episodic memory recalls the sunset on that beach and the sand on my knee as my future wife read the last line of the poem, "Will you marry me?" These semantic and episodic memories are stored.

Retrieval cues

To be retrieved from storage, cues play an essential role. A cue is essentially anything (such as a physical object, situation, time period, word, question, concept, etc.,) which is paired with a memory trace. The cue triggers retrieval of the memory. The more cues, the more likely the retrieval. No memory exists in isolation as it is part of a network of associations and cues. A cue may by the first letter of a word that brings the word to mind. For instance, name a flower that starts with the letter "b" and you would start to think of begonias or buttercups. A cue works very poorly with the last letter of a word; the last letter does not trigger association. As designer of human memory, God employs cues as tools to help you remember rightly and retrieve memories that accomplish the original pre-fall uncorrupted divine design for memory, to glorify and enjoy the Creator.

SENSORY CUES

In the garage, many projects required multiple steps and multiple tools for each step. To replace the brakes on the car, the lineup of tools included everything from Allen wrenches, socket wrenches, sockets, a jack stand and lift, to name a few. Each tool provided an important function to complete the job. Nothing would send work in the garage to a screeching halt like a stripped bolt that was impossible to grip and loosen. My dad would call me over to help. I would end up holding a wrench while he used other tools in the garage, other wrenches and even the hammer, until the bolt finally was removed. It a multi-hand and multi-tool event.

God uses the cues from your five senses, touch, smell, taste, sight, and sound, to help your dysfunctional memory. These senses each closely work with your memory to store, retrieve, and reorient you back to Him. These five senses many times act together and not in isolation as many things you experience are multisensory. The senses overlap and work in tandem.

John, the disciple whom Jesus loved, credited the senses as the groundwork for the gospel and its proclamation. He testified that "what we have heard, what we have seen with our eyes, what we have looked at and touched with our hands, concerning the Word of Life" (1 John 1:1) was proclaimed so that others may also believe and fellowship with Christ. John's eyewitness account was based on his five senses and drove his desire to share the good news.

THE CUE OF TOUCH (HAPTIC)

Touch (also called haptic perception) strongly relates to your body's awareness of its movement and place in space. Haptic memory associates touch with specific recall of certain memories in complex ways. In a recent experiment, study participants were blindfolded and explored 168 common everyday objects.[3] The participant then was presented with the object he felt and a second similar object, like two pens, and had to decide which one he had touched in the blindfolded test. Even after one week, participants identified the object correctly 85 percent of the time.

Belief
....

Touch impacts memory in ways not fully understood by science. In the Bible, John provided a climactic account of how Christ used touch to strengthen belief. Following His resurrection, Jesus appeared to the disciples and "showed them both His hands and His side" (John 20:21). The disciples rejoiced and believed as they touched His hands and side, recalling the details of His death in these scars; but Thomas was not with them. Despite the other ten disciples' report, Thomas declared his doubt would only dissolve if he himself saw and touched Christ's hand and side. Jesus ap-

3 Fabian Hutmacher and Kuhbandner Christof, "Long-Term Memory for Haptically Explored Objects: Fidelity, Durability, Incidental Encoding, and Cross-Modal Transfer," *Psychological science* vol. 29,12 (2018), 2031–38.

peared again and met Thomas right at his point of need to help his unbelief. Thomas exclaimed, "My Lord, and my God!" (John 20:28). Christ was "pierced through for our transgressions" (Isa. 53:5) and yet He was alive!

Pain
....

Touch also closely associates with pain. Acute pain is necessary but unwanted. When you touch a hot surface, your hand recoils to avoid an even greater injury. As a child, you quickly learn what to avoid as you experience what is hot and cold, sharp and dull. In fact, your body contains different nociceptors (pain receptors). *Noci* is from Latin that means "hurt," and these receptors activate for different types of pain from heat, pressure, and chemicals.[4] These receptors can malfunction and be turned on chronically.

All pain, acute or chronic, is unwanted as no one likes to experience pain, but acute pain serves as a tutor to teach what is safe and not safe. Pain lodges into memory and even enhances memory for an event. God purposefully uses pain for your good in the form of discipline to guide you back onto the right path so "that we may share his holiness. For the moment all discipline seems painful rather than pleasant, but later it yields the peaceful fruit of righteousness to those who have been trained by it" (Heb. 12:10–11). The pain directs you back in the present to Him and serves as a warning in the future.

As an emergency medicine doctor, one of the main initial elements of treatment is pain relief with the goal to minimize discomfort and suffering; but pain is necessary to alert to danger and trigger you to seek help to prevent further injury. In the emergency room, many patients seek help for chest pain. With an EKG and blood tests, a heart attack can be detected quickly. Time is important, as the faster the diagnosis is made, the faster the cardiologist (heart specialist) is able to stent open the blocked blood vessels that are decreasing blood flow and oxygen to the heart, damaging the muscle. However, some heart attacks do not produce any pain and are called silent. The patient stays at

4 D. Purves, G. J. Augustine, D. Fitzpatrick, et al., eds. Neuroscience, 2nd ed. (Sunderland (MA): Sinauer Associates, 2001).

home unaware as the heart muscle is injured. Pain produces the urgency to seek help.

Pain, physical and emotional, directs the Christian to seek out the Great Physician. "Christ is a physician good at all diseases, especially the binding of a broken heart."[5] Do not be like King Asa who "became diseased in his feet. His disease was severe, yet even in his disease he did not seek the LORD, but the physicians" (2 Chron. 16:12). Touch—and particularly pain— unpleasantly but necessarily direct the mind and heart back to God.

THE CUE OF SMELL (OLFACTORY)

Smell is a very strong cue, highly resistant to forgetting. Research shows that smells activate a pathway directly to the hippocampus, the part of your brain responsible for long-term memory.[6] Armed with about four hundred types of olfactory (smell) receptors, the nose can detect up to one trillion different odors.[7] In my childhood, the smell of car oil would take me back to the garage and oil changes on the 1978 Subaru. After the car accident in 2005, a box arrived with the salvaged belongings of my family. When opening the box, the smell of car oil hit my nose. I will never forget it; and each time I open up one of the recovered Bibles, the smell hits as I turn the pages. Through those difficult but sweet times of reading the Bibles and the notes, the smell no longer prompts sadness and a pit in my stomach, but rather thankfulness—thankfulness for treasured and wise words written inside the covers of the Bible like "Will I trust God if he never tells me why?" Associations with a smell may change over time, but the cues are powerful.

God uses these powerful cues to bring you back to Him. An example is first seen in Exodus 30 where God gives Moses the recipe for incense made of spices in equal parts. This incense was not to be used for everyday perfume as this mixture was

5 Richard Sibbes, *The Bruised Reed* (Edinburgh: The Banner of Truth Trust, 1998), 8.

6 University of Toronto. "Scientists uncover new connection between smell and memory: Findings offer opportunities for improved smell tests in Alzheimer's disease diagnosis." ScienceDaily, 23 July, 2018.

7 Sarah Williams, "Human nose can detect a trillion smells," 20 March, 2014, Web. 11 September, 2020, sciencemag.org.

holy to God and was to be burned perpetually before the Lord to "remind" God of His covenant and "remind" the people of God's holiness. Today, believers no longer burn incense to God and sacrifice burnt offerings. Instead, the believing church is now "a fragrance of Christ to God" (2 Cor. 2:15). How is this possible? Because Christ loved you and "gave Himself up for you, an offering and sacrifice to God as a fragrant aroma" (Eph. 5:2). Let the sense of smell remind you to worship God, then, by walking in love, and let the sweet aroma of Christ spread to all those around you as a witness to the world. The love of Christ is unique, identifiable, and a pleasant aroma to God and others.

THE CUE OF TASTE (GUSTATORY)

God also uses the sense of taste to redirect your mind back to Him. About ten thousand taste buds cover the human tongue in a fairly even distribution except in the very middle, which has none. With a life expectancy of ten days, taste buds regenerate quickly, which is how you rapidly recover from burning your tongue on hot soup. Taste buds detect sweet, salty, sour, bitter, and umami (savory flavor). Taste elicits emotional responses ranging from enjoyment to disgust.

God refers to taste in reference to His Word that is "sweeter than honey" (Ps. 119:103) and "the drippings of the honeycomb" (Ps. 19:10). One of our family friends kept a beehive and would bring samples of honeycomb for us to try. The sweetness of honeycomb overwhelms and provides a great analogy to the Word. But God also uses bitter taste. For the Passover meal, God commanded that the Israelites eat the unblemished roasted lamb with bitter herbs (Ex. 12:8). The bitter herbs served as a reminder to the Israelites of the past in Egypt with "lives bitter with hard labor" (Ex. 1:14). God maximizes His design of taste to help refocus your mind through things as diverse as sweet honeycomb and bitter herbs.

THE CUE OF SIGHT (VISUAL)

God created man with eyes that connect the world visually to memory through the optic nerve, a bundle of around one million neurons.[8] Vision depends on the fovea, a spot that measures smaller than a pinhead. The fovea contains a dense group of rods and cones, photoreceptors that are responsible for vision in low light (rods) and color (cones). Cones help your eye distinguish up to ten million different colors.[9] These components of the eye create a powerful aid to memory with recognition of brightness, pattern, shape, and color.[10]

For obedience
••••••••••••••••••

A picture is worth a thousand words because a picture helps you remember those thousand words. "Hear a piece of information and three days later you'll remember 10 percent of it. Add a picture and you'll remember 65 percent."[11] Using these visual cues, God commanded Moses to keep a jar of manna for future generations to "see the bread that I fed you in the wilderness, when I brought you out of Egypt" (Ex. 16:32). The manna in the jar did not spoil; the delicate white flakes were there as a visual reminder of God's provision. God also helped the people with another simple visual aid as the people made tassels for the corners of their garments with a cord of blue "for you to look at and remember all the commandments of the LORD, so as to do them and not follow after your own heart and your own eyes" (Num. 15:39).

8 H. Kolb, "Facts and Figures Concerning the Human Retina," 1 May, 2005 [Updated 5 July, 2007], in "Webvision: The Organization of the Retina and Visual System" [Internet], eds. H. Kolb, E. Fernandez, R. Nelson (Salt Lake City, UT: University of Utah Health Sciences Center, 1995).

9 Deane B. Judd and Günter Wyszecki, *Color in Business, Science and Industry* (1975). Wiley Series in Pure and Applied Optics (3rd ed.) (New York: Wiley-Interscience), 388.

10 Alan Baddeley, *Essentials of Human Memory* (Psychology Press, 2014), 11.

11 John Medina, "Rule #10." Brain rules.net.

For restraint

Combat visual temptation with a visual reminder to obey God's commandments. Korah led a rebellion against Moses and Aaron that ended with God's judgment of those who rebelled. Eleazar, the son of Aaron, took the bronze censers of these rebel priests and hammered out a covering for the altar "to be a reminder to the people of Israel, so that no outsider, who is not of the descendants of Aaron, should draw near to burn incense before the LORD, lest he become like Korah and his company" (Num. 16:40). When a future high priest would go to sacrifice an offering to God, the bronze censers of rebellion would catch the light of the fire and glow to remind the high priest of God's holiness and justice.

For perpetuity

Monuments compose another form of a visual aid. Monuments are constructed to remind of a person or event and generally are designed out of material that will endure beyond the present generation. God used monuments to help the people of Israel remember. Following forty years of wandering in the wilderness, God piled up the water of the Jordan River for Israel to cross over into the Promised Land, a fresh start that resembled the first start with the parting of the Red Sea. After the crossing of the Jordan, God commanded Joshua to select a man from each tribe to go back into the water and select a stone from the middle of the river bed where the priests were standing with the ark (Josh. 4:3–5). These stones were set up by Joshua at Gilgal (Josh. 4:20) for a purpose. "When your children ask their fathers in time to come, saying 'What are these stones?' Then you shall inform your children saying, 'Israel crossed the Jordan on dry ground'" (Josh. 4:21–22). Joshua went on to explain that the Jordan crossing must be remembered so that "all the peoples of the earth may know that the hand of the LORD is mighty, so that you may fear the LORD your God forever" (Josh. 4:24). Sadly, soon after the death of Joshua—even with this monument—Israel turned to idolatry at Gilgal. Later in future generations, Gilgal was specifically mentioned by Amos and Hosea for its famed transgression. Hosea condemned

Gilgal for their sacrifices on altars "like the stone heaps beside the furrows of the field" (Hos. 12:11). The memorial stones of the Jordan were forgotten amidst the many stones of idolatrous altars.

For redirection

A monument is built to stand the test of time; but the monument not only must physically remain but also its message be remembered. Monuments serve for your education and not just veneration. The Puritan Philip Doddridge prayed, "And may we one day join in a nobler and more immediate worship where all the symbols and shadows will be laid aside—where even these memorials are no longer needed."[12] For the Christian, these memorials remind us like Samuel's stone monument, Ebenezer, that "the LORD has helped us" (1 Sam. 7:12). Hymn writer Robert Robinson in *Come Thou Fount of Every Blessing* captured this imagery with the lyrics,

> *Here I raise my Ebenezer*
> *Hither by thy help I've come*
> *And I hope, by Thy good pleasure*
> *Safely to arrive at home.*[13]

These visual aids provided by God keep redirecting you back to Him so that He is not out of sight, and thus not out of mind.

THE CUE OF HEARING (AUDITORY)

Hearing relies on the three smallest bones in your body—the only bones that do not grow in your lifetime. These bones do not bear any weight but amplify the sound waves that hit your ear drum (tympanic membrane). These bones strike a structure that looks like a snail called the cochlea filled with fluid that moves 2,700 small hairs. The movement of these tiny hairs send signals down the auditory nerve to the brain. What a complex task for a structure that could sit on a coin the size of a quarter.

12 Philip Doddridge, "A prayer to prepare for communion," *Piercing Heaven: Prayers of the Puritans,* ed. Robert Elmer (Lexham Press, 2019), 143.

13 Robert Robinson, "Come Thou Fount of Every Blessing."

Hearing plays a significant role in short-term memory, which is why you are able to remember a longer string of numbers by not just reading but saying them out loud; but hearing also greatly impacts your long-term memory. In fact, ancient cultures, and even some today, rely on oral records to pass on traditions. Oral records preceded written records. Even now in cultures that have written records, listening is key as the written record is read (1 Tim. 4:13). Hearing happens continuously even during sleep, but listening requires undivided attention.

Speaking

Speaking is another miracle important for communication. Speech and language involve the lips, tongue, larynx (voice box), lungs, nerves, and the brain. Speech and language can easily be damaged and lost when one small blood clot causes a stroke in one of two small language centers of the brain (called Wernicke's and Broca's). If Wernicke's area is damaged, you lose language comprehension but will still be able to speak words. The words topple out like a word salad, a string of words that do not belong together like "ghost I green the stinky hugs they pies." If Broca's area is damaged, the patient can understand words but cannot speak them at all. Damage to either language center debilitates communication. These finely tuned systems are taken for granted until they are disrupted.

Generational sharing

God endowed humans with the remarkable gift of hearing and speaking to pass along information to the next generation for the purpose of glorifying God (Ps. 71:18). "One generation shall commend Your works to another, and shall declare Your mighty acts" (Ps. 145:4). The younger generation needs the corporate testimony of the older generation.

In 1993, a severe drought plagued Tanzania's Tarangine National Park. As the usual water sources dried up, the scientists observed three elephant herds.[14] One herd led by a younger

14 Charles Foley, Nathalie Pettorelli, and Lara Foley, "2008 Severe drought and calf survival in elephants," *Biology Letters.* 4: 541–544.

matriarch stayed put while two herds with older matriarchs left the parched park. The herd that stayed put suffered higher losses of their newborn calves. The researchers observed that the herds that left the park for other water sources were led by matriarchs who had survived the previous drought from 1958 to 1961. These older matriarchs recalled the prior water sources from over thirty years ago and guided their herds to safety. The younger generation benefits from the wisdom of the older generation in ways that should not be overlooked.

Parental teaching

God uses the memory of hearing to learn specifically from parents. Parents play a central role in passing down the truth. Parents are commanded to teach the commandments "diligently to your sons and shall talk of them when you sit in your house and when you walk by the way and when you lie down and when you rise up" (Deut. 6:7). If you think this is only important for Israel and not the early church, look at Timothy who listened to his grandmother Lois and his mother Eunice who passed down the legacy of faith to him (2 Tim. 1:5). Timothy heard and believed. "Faith comes from hearing, and hearing by the word of Christ" (Rom. 10:17).

Preaching

The importance of listening in memory not only includes the parent but also the preacher. Preachers are the Lord's remembrancers as "all biblical preaching in the context of the worship service is an act of reminding."[15] As the listener sits under the preaching of God's Word, the mind does not stop at remembering but responds in conviction (Heb. 4:12), restoration (Ps. 19:7), wisdom (Ps. 19:7), joy (Ps. 19:8), growth (1 Peter 2:2), and maturity (1 Thess. 2:13). Listening is not in one ear and out the other but rather enters the ear, deposits in the mind, quickens the affections, and matures the soul. The preacher beckons the weary and distracted to listen and remember the truths

15 Jeffrey Arthurs, *Preaching as Reminding* (InterVarsity Press, 2017), 48.

that have been drowned out during the week. Humility listens while love speaks. Truly, the ears are the gateway to the mind.

THE CUE OF MUSIC

Closely connected to hearing, music is another cue that God has given to help people remember rightly. God sings (Zeph. 3:17) and humans bearing His image sing to Him. Singing involves the mind and not just the lips. Interestingly, God created long-term memory for music to be stored outside of the hippocampus (the main place for other long-term memories).[16] This is why musical memory remains in Alzheimers when many other functions of memory fade. In a memory-care facility at Christmas, a sweet lady in her eighties kept asking my daughter her name every few minutes; but when the piano started playing, she knew every word of *Away in a Manger*.

As I was growing up, music played an important role in my family. My dad received a master's degree in music composition from the University of Washington while my mom also played clarinet. I grew up singing songs in church that my dad wrote. But the music that had the most lasting impact on my life were the psalms he set to music. Despite learning these psalms over thirty years ago, I still am able to sing Psalm 32 and 34 from memory. What an amazing gift that combines musical memory and Scripture memory!

Theological
· · · · · · · · · · · · · · · ·

Beyond just remembering words, singing provides a medium to echo your theology back to God and lay hold of His promises. The first song in the Bible, the song of Moses, proclaimed theology as the Israelites stood on the banks of the Red Sea rejoicing in God's victory over the Egyptian army. The first song reverberates in Psalm 118 that quotes the song of Moses, "The LORD is my strength and my song, and He has become my salvation" (Ex.

16 Esfahani-Bayerl, Nazli et al. "Musical memory and hippocampus revisited: Evidence from a musical layperson with highly selective hippocampal damage," *Cortex; a journal devoted to the study of the nervous system and behavior*, vol. 119 (2019): 519–527.

15:2; Ps. 118:14). As part of the Hallel, Psalm 118 was sung by the Israelites as part of the ancient Passover tradition, and that tradition would have been a part of the event in the upper room with Jesus and His disciples. Matthew recorded, "After singing a hymn, they went out to the Mount of Olives" (Matt. 26:30). Jesus sang the lyric from the song of Moses as He walked the way to the cross to accomplish salvation mentioned in the song. The song of Moses was not only sung by David and Christ but also will be sung in the future in heaven. John recorded a future scene in heaven when the victorious people of God will sing the song of Moses and the song of the Lamb (Rev. 15:3–4). The redemption of Israel from Egypt will culminate in worship of the final redemption of God's people. Music is an excellent cue for memory that passes along the words of worship from the first song in the Bible to the last song.

Congregational

As seen with the song of Moses, music unites generationally. Music effectively transfers truths from one generation to the next. "Hymns unite the past to the present and forge our faith as we recognize the unity through generations of the common foundations of theology we share in Christ."[17] I grew up singing hymns, and now I see how these hymns kept instilling in me the gospel over and over again. A hymn will bring up the problem of sin in the first verse and then proceed to the work of redemption at the cross in the second verse. The last verse ends with a look forward to future triumph and glorification.[18] As the congregation sings these words of theology back to God, the mind anchors deeper into the bedrock of unity in truth.

Unity in song reminds me of the fireflies I would catch in a jar at my aunt's house on humid summer nights. How did the fireflies synchronize their glow? Scientists discovered each firefly possesses its own internal clock; when the clock strikes "midnight," the firefly glows. These clocks, though, are adjustable, and each firefly, little by little, adjusts its clock to match its

17 Jared C. Wilson, "The gospel of the kingdom is like an old hymn," 13 July 2016, Web. 11 September, 2020, thegospelcoalition.org.

18 Ibid.

neighbor's clock until all are in sync. Singing theological truths sync the individuals in a church to unify in a gospel glow to the world. Singing is "speaking to one another" (Eph. 5:19) from the overflow of the "words of Christ that dwell richly within you" (Col. 3:16). Ultimately, the purpose of memory and purpose of music sing the same melody of worshipping God.

THE CUE OF SPATIAL MEMORY

Worship is not confined to within the church walls, but God provides a place of worship that further assists in rightly remembering. Spatial memory, memory by location and relation of spaces between objects, involves input from all five senses. Spatial memory involves a part of the brain called the parietal lobes (top part of your brain). Spatial memory strongly links memory to its surrounding context. An old trick to trigger your memory is to go back to the original place the memory was formed. The place triggers neuronal firing that ignites the closely associated memory trace.

The place of worship plays a pivotal role in remembrance. The worship building is "the ductus of the soul" that flows directly to God.[19] The mind regains a right focus when entering into the worship place. Asaph picked up on this reorientation of the mind when he struggled with the prosperity of the wicked. He questioned if God noticed his plight and then abruptly shifted when he "came into the sanctuary of God; then I perceived their end" (Ps. 73:17). Asaph went on to confess his embittered and ignorant heart. He entered the place of worship, and his mind reoriented from questioning God to worshiping God. Place oriented Asaph back to a right theology of who God is. A place of worship rekindled worship. Today's church building serves not only as a place to draw out worship to God on Sunday but also as a place for life events. The church building serves as a place to celebrate births, baptisms, and weddings, but also a place to ponder death in funerals. Place provides the space to orient back to Him.

19 Mary Carruthers, *The Craft of Thought* (Cambridge University Press, 2000), 254.

EPISODIC MEMORY CUES

God not only provides tools and cues for memory; He also gives you powerful events to help you remember rightly. Episodic memory, memory of specific events, adds action to the tools and cues. "Adding the action dimension seems to make recall far more resistant to effects of time and aging."[20] Action enriches the memory and makes it easily accessible.

Episodic memory intertwines with emotional memory, which is stored in the amygdala. The amygdala's name originates from the Latin word for "almond" due its almondlike shape. When an event takes place, you not only remember the event, but the emotions attached to it like the joy of a wedding. However, you may re-remember the same event with different emotions.[21] Instead of a source of joy, the event is now a source of sadness.

The Sabbath

The first event God established at the culmination of creation was the Sabbath. God commanded Israel to "remember the sabbath day, to keep it holy" (Ex. 20:8). God rested on the seventh day not because He needed to rest but to provide an example for humanity who needs rest. At present, God is actively moving and working all the time as "He never slumbers or sleeps" (Ps. 121:1). God is the only one who never rests, while all creatures require sleep. Rest, though, is not just sleep but rather a ceasing of labor to refresh, refocus, and worship. Busyness drowns out the condition of the mind. The Sabbath reorients the week. The repetitious renewal of the mind is vital for right remembrance.

Feasts and celebrations

Repeated celebrations incorporate an active remembrance. In the Pentateuch, God established these feasts for the purpose of remembering. The feast of unleavened bread, called a memorial (Ex. 12:14), reminded the Israelites of the night they left Egypt in

20 Alan Baddeley, *Essentials of Human Memory* (Psychology Press, 2014), 162.

21 John Swinton, *Dementia: Living in the Memories of God* (Eerdmans Publishing Co., 2012), 208.

haste without time to leaven the bread (Deut. 16:3). The Feast of Weeks focused around provision in the wheat harvest with the purpose to "remember that you were a slave in Egypt" (Deut. 16:12). At the end of the harvest of grapes in the fall, Israel celebrated the Feast of Booths. The Israelites would build booths to live in for seven days to celebrate "so that generations may know that I had the sons of Israel live in booths when I brought them from the land of Egypt" (Lev. 23:43). For all three feasts, God pointed Israel back to their redemption from Egypt while they praised God for His provision.

All of these celebrations actively engaged the people in a way that might be foreign in Western culture. "In our Western (Greek) intellectual heritage, 'remembering' means 'recollecting': recalling to mind something that is no longer a present reality. Nothing could be further from a Jewish conception. For example, in the Jewish liturgy, 'remembering' means participating here and now in certain defining events in the past and also in the future."[22] Baking bread, harvesting wheat and grapes, and building booths engaged the senses and enabled the participant to experience the past in the present.

Passover

The pinnacle celebration of remembrance in the Old Testament is the Passover. Passover marked the salvation and birth of the nation—so much so that God started the calendar year at that point as "this month will be the beginning of months for you." To assist memory, God included instructions for active participation and obedience. Each household purchased an unblemished one-year-old male lamb on the tenth day of the month and kept the lamb in the house until the fourteenth day when the lamb was slain. The blood of the lamb would be placed on the doorposts and lintel (header across the door frame). On the first Passover, the blood served as a sign of obedience for the occupants of the house (Ex. 12:13). Finally, the lamb would be prepared without any bones broken, roasted, and eaten with unleavened bread and bitter herbs.

God clearly gave the purpose for the Passover. When children

22 Michael Horton, *The Christian Faith: A Systematic Theology for Pilgrims on the Way* (Zondervan Academic, 2011), 799.

of future generations ask, "'What does this rite mean to you?' You shall say, 'It is Passover sacrifice to the LORD who passed over the houses of the sons of Israel in Egypt when He smote the Egyptians, but spared our homes'" (Ex. 12:26–27). The purpose is not to simply pass information on to the next generation who did not experience the actual events, but to engage the future generation in active participation in the events. Ross Blackburn observes,

> The ceremonies draw future generations and the events of the Exodus together, so that Israel's descendants might, through ritual, participate in the Egyptian deliverance. In each case, the Israelites are bidden to re-enact an event that happened on the night of the Exodus....The purpose of this ritual re-enactment, however, is not simply to remember a past event through drama, but rather to bring the past and the present together for subsequent generations.[23]

The Passover strengthened the event in the mind by taking the participants back to Egypt to share in the event where God powerfully worked. The purpose of remembering the Passover was worship and obedience, not only for the Israelites who were present but also for future generations.

Passover accomplished a renewal of the individual and corporate mind toward God, a realignment of memory back to its original design to worship God. But the most important Passover in the Bible occurs in the New Testament when the Lamb of God celebrated the Last Supper with His disciples.

LORD'S TABLE

The Lamb of God

The Last Supper linked the Old Covenant Passover to the New Covenant communion. Not only did the Last Supper occur on Passover (Matt. 26:19), but many other features connect the former with the present practice. The Passover lamb was prepared without any broken bones; and, similarly, Christ the

23 W. Ross Blackburn, *The God Who Makes Himself Known* (IVP Academic, 2013), 51.

Lamb was sacrificed without any of His bones broken (Ps. 34:20; John 19:36). Also, Christ's blood was poured out on the wooden beams of the cross, a similar image of the Passover lamb's blood spread on the doorposts and lintel. Effectively, Christ's blood covered over sin as God passed over the guilty who believe.

The Bread and Cup

As an important contrast to the Passover, Christ did not command the future remembrance of His death to include a lamb, but rather bread and wine. Why? Because the Lamb of God paid for sins once and for all. The church no longer sacrifices a lamb at the Lord's Table but rather remembers the all-sufficient sacrifice of Christ through the bread and cup. The Lord's Table clearly looked back to the past Passover but also now looks forward to the marriage supper of the Lamb (Rev. 19:9). Jesus directed the disciples' minds to the future as He said, "I will not drink of the fruit of the vine from now on until that day when I drink it new with you in my Father's Kingdom" (Matt. 26:29). The Lord's Table leverages memory of the covenant-keeping God of the past to build hope and faith for the future fulfillment as "we eagerly await Him" (Heb. 9:28).

The Necessity

The Lord's Table is the foremost aid of episodic memory provided by God to the church today. "Do this in remembrance of Me" (Luke 17:19). God knows that a distorted memory needs help; and He gave the church a means to reorient rightly in a repetitive and regular fashion. "The frequency of it is to show how often we need to be reminded of our dear Lord, for we are prone to forget him."[24] Treacherous memory "can recollect anything but Christ, and forget nothing so easy as him whom we ought to remember? While memory will preserve a poisoned weed, it suffereth the Rose of Sharon to with-

24 Charles H. Spurgeon, "The Lord's Supper: a remembrance of Jesus." 19 August, 1888, Web. 24 August, 2020, spurgeon.org.

er."[25] Corrupted memory requires help from the Holy Spirit through means like the Lord's Table to redirect back to God and remember rightly.

The types of memory

So how does God specifically utilize the Lord's Table to renew remembrance? God marvelously activates all types of memory previously discussed. Semantic memory—knowledge of facts— plays a role as the believer remembers the historical facts of the death and resurrection of Jesus. Episodic memory brings to mind events as each Lord's Table itself is an event to commemorate the event of the cross. Procedural memory—the knowledge of how to do things—activates with the participatory style of the Lord's Table to take, eat, and drink.

The multisensory experience

God fully engages the believer's memory at all levels with the use of all five senses. A participant in the Lord's Table picks up the cup and the bread, smells the contents of the cup as it is lifted to the mouth, sees and tastes the bread, and hears the words and music that accompany. "Thus the senses, which are usually clogs to the soul, become wings to lift the mind in contemplation."[26] This multisensory episodic remembrance activates your mind, the parietal lobe (touch), occipital lobe (vision), temporal lobe (hearing), frontal lobe (taste), and limbic system (smell), all to help the believer remember rightly. God who designed memory knows how to use it. "Those in multi-sensory environments always do better than those in uni-sensory environments. They have more recall with better resolution that lasts longer, evident even 20 years later."[27] Christ does not just command the church to do this in remembrance but also provides the best way to do so.

25 Charles H. Spurgeon, "The remembrance of Christ," 7 January, 1855, Web. 24 August, 2020, spurgeon.org.

26 Ibid.

27 John Medina, "Rule #9." Brain rules.net.

The Emotions
••••••••••••••••••

By stirring memory through the senses, the Lord's Table not only recalls to mind the history of Christ's death and resurrection but draws out "an affectionate remembrance" that "when we so call Christ and his death to our minds as to feel the powerful impressions thereof upon our hearts."[28] The affections will be moved to hate sin as you remember the cost of your sin; but the affections will also move in an abounding love for the Savior Himself. The Lord's Table pushes the memory beyond just the action and to the Person. "Do this in remembrance of ME" (Luke 22:19, emphasis added). "It is Christ's glorious person which ought to be the object of our remembrance."[29] You can know many historical facts and doctrines about Jesus but do you actually know Him?[30] The object of the Lord's Table is not just to examine self but to know and love your Savior. "For every look at self, take ten looks at Christ."[31] The Lord's Table redirects the mind off of self and back into relationship and worship of God.

28 John Flavel, *The Fountain of Life* (Monergism Books, 2015), 267.

29 Charles H. Spurgeon, "The remembrance of Christ," 7 January, 1855, Web. 24 August, 2020, spurgeon.org.

30 Charles H. Spurgeon, "The Lord's Supper: a remembrance of Jesus," 19 August, 1888, Web. 24 August, 2020, spurgeon.org.

31 Andrew Bonar, *Memoirs and Remains of the Rev. Robert Murray McCheyne* (The Banner of Truth Trust, 1966), 293.

Chapter 6
Application Questions

1. In what ways can pain be harmful, and in what ways can pain be helpful?

2. How did God use smell and taste to help Israel remember rightly? Do you have any good memories associated with a smell or taste? Write them down.

3. Do you have any visual aids around your house that help reorient your memory back to God? What would be some further ways to add visual reminders to your everyday life?

4. How does music help us to remember truth? How does music connect past and present generations?

5. Why is the Lord's Table the pinnacle of remembrance? How do the senses play a role in the Lord's Table?

7

The Keys of Redemptive Memory

The garage door separated the smells of the workshop from the smells of the bakeshop. Swinging open the door to enter the kitchen, I found the smell of car oil would be replaced by the smell of funnel cakes frying in hot oil. My mom was known inside and outside our home as an excellent cook. Each of us children longed to not just eat but also make her food; but it turned out the eating was much easier than the making. Each child would attempt to make particular favorites like mine, chicken pot pie. The key to success sat in a small, flowered box, marked "recipes." Shuffling through the cards stained with past ingredients and filled with secrets passed from generation to generation, I found the recipe I was searching for. If I followed the recipe, the hope was that the pie would turn out like all the past delicious pies before it. However, I needed assistance. My mom would collect all the ingredients and the tools to measure, cut, and stir. But even with the instructions written out and all the ingredients, I still needed help from my mom, who would gently oversee and guide my measuring, cutting, and stirring. Without my mom, the instructions would be impossible for me to follow and make the savory pot pie.

In a similar way, God has written down commands for His people to remember and follow. The commands to remember are important, so much so that God graciously provides all the Christian needs to follow obediently and carry out the recipe. The Christian views these commands with hope—hope that the commands will accomplish the end goal of pleasing Him. God emphasizes the importance of the commands to remember by the sheer number of them (over 200). One of these commands says, "Remember also your Creator in the days of your youth, before the evil days come and the years draw near when you will say, 'I have no delight in them'" (Eccl. 12:1). Remember when you are young. The recipes you first learned are the least forgotten.

THE PROMISES

Pilgrim's Progress teaches another important facet of God's commands. Christian and Hopeful sat in Doubting Castle, wounded from the cudgel of Giant Despair. At the lowest point, they knelt down and began to pray at midnight. While praying with dawn fast approaching, Christian stopped and cried out, "What a fool I am to lie in a stinking dungeon, when I may as well walk at liberty! I have a key in my bosom, called Promise, that will, I am persuaded, open any lock in Doubting Castle." So he put his hand into his shirt, plucked out the key, and thrust it into the lock; and the key opened the door. The two pilgrims opened the gate, which creaked and woke up the giant; and yet, Despair could not capture them.[1] Free at last!

The memory that wielded the cudgel and inflicted them with shame and guilt now aided their rescue, bringing to mind the key of the precious promises of God. God's commands to remember are bracketed not only by His provisions but also His promises. Without His provision and promise, the commands weigh you down with self-reliance. God's promises remove the burden and point back to reliance upon Him.

Peter clarifies that God's "divine power has granted to us everything pertaining to life and godliness through the true knowledge of Him who called us by His own glory and excellence.

1 John Bunyan, The Pilgrim's Progress (London: Gall and Inglis, undated), 154–56.

For by these, He has granted to us His precious promises, so that by them you may become partakers of the divine nature" (2 Peter 1:3–4). God's promises are not "pie crust promises, easily made and easily broken."[2] His promises are an inexhaustible treasure. The Christian "is already privileged as a king with the silver key that unlocks the strong room; he may even grasp the scepter, wear the crown, and put on his shoulders the imperial mantle."[3] These promises of God outweigh, outmeasure, and outlast the problems of man. The commands are melted down together with His provision and promises to form the key. In this cross-shaped key, you will find both the indicative (what God has done for you through Christ) and the imperative (what a believer is called to do). The key sits close by in your pocket, and yet is easily forgotten.

THE COMMANDS

So what are these commands that God specifically calls you to remember? In examining the commands, they will be organized by the object of the command: God, you, others, and the Bible. These four groups of commands never stray far from provision and promise.

REMEMBER GOD

In the recipe to remember, the place to start is the command "Remember the LORD your God" (Deut. 8:18). This is absolutely critical. "What comes into our minds when we think about God is the most important thing about us."[4] Thoughts of God influence all of life. God gives commands to remember Him because He knows how important He is. It is only by remembering Him that we can truly be satisfied.

How do you remember God? The command in isolation sounds austere and difficult to do. The psalmist recorded his own private remembrance of this command. "When I remember You on my

2 A line from Mary Poppins, *Mary Poppins Returns,* 2018.

3 Charles H. Spurgeon, *Gleanings among the Sheaves* (New York: Fleming B. Revell, 1869), 5–6.

4 A. W. Tozer, *The Knowledge of the Holy* (HarperCollins, 1961), 1.

bed, I meditate on You in the night watches, for You have been my help, and in the shadow of Your wings I sing for joy. My soul clings to You; Your right hand upholds me" (Ps. 63:6–8). David's memory drove his worship relationally. David did not just recall things about a God but sang and clung to His God that He knew personally. Use your memory to gain a fuller picture of who God is, and what His attributes are.

Remember God's actions

Who God is closely links to what He does. His actions reveal His character and prove His promises are true. To know the mighty deeds of the God of the Bible is to know the deeds of your God today. Meditate on the ancient acts of God in the past to find comfort in the present because the God of the ancient past is the same God in the present. He is the same yesterday, today, and forever (Ps. 102:25–27). How easy it is to forget that the God who parted the Red Sea is my God, your God.

Remember how He redeemed you. "Forget none of His benefits; who pardons all your iniquities, who heals all your diseases, who redeems your life from the pit, who crowns you with lovingkindness and compassion, who satisfies your years with good things so that your youth is renewed like the eagle" (Ps. 103:2–5). All of the power on display at the Red Sea salvation now applies to you in personal redemption. The same God who parted the Red Sea pardoned your sin.

Remember God's Son

Today, Christians experience these benefits through Christ. The commands to remember culminate with "Remember Jesus Christ, risen from the dead, descendant of David" (1 Tim. 2:8). The key to memory resides here. The person of Christ not only redeemed memory at the cross, but He also provides the promise for future and final victory in the resurrection from the dead. When do you need to remember Christ, who He is and what He has done? At all times, but here specifically Paul implored Timothy to remember Christ in the midst of suffering (1 Tim. 2:3). Paul remembered Christ as he suffered for Christ (1 Tim. 2:9–10). For those who have suffered (or will suffer) in the past, present, or future, remember Christ. Why consider and meditate on Christ in suffering? Because Christ suffered greatly, even though He was sinless. Remember the One who suffered for you as you suffer for Him.

REMEMBER YOURSELF

Remember your suffering

The writer of Hebrews called his audience to "remember the former days, when, after being enlightened, you endured great conflict of sufferings partly by being made a public spectacle through reproaches and tribulations, and partly by becoming sharers with those who were so treated" (Heb. 10:32–33). So, why is it better for these Christians to remember their suffering rather than erase it? Wouldn't it be better to not have any recall of this pain or the potential to relive it?

Would anything be lost by erasing all suffering from memory? First, the sufferer loses the benefits of growing. Suffering and growth appear contradictory; however, suffering does not banish growth, but gives opportunity to bolster it. In suffering, you survey the past like Christian in *The Pilgrim's Progress* who traveled through the valley of the shadow of death. The sun rose and "he looked back, not out of a desire to return, but to see by the light of the day what hazards he had gone through in the dark."[5] Christian responded by singing praises to God for his deliverance.

The sufferer loses the full joy of triumph if He erases his suffering. In fact, the sufferer would lose the opportunity to fully worship God, the primary purpose of memory. God uses the darkness of suffering to better shine a light on His good handiwork. "Providence is best read like Hebrew, backwards! Only then is it possible to trace the divine hand on the tiller guiding the Gospel ship into a safe harbor. No matter how dark things get, His hand is always in control."[6] Suffering strains the purpose of memory;

5 John Bunyan, *The Pilgrim's Progress* (London: Gall and Inglis, undated), 88.

6 John Flavel, *The Mystery of Providence,* Web. 15 October, 2020, monergism.com.

it forces the sufferer to reckon with God and who He is. As my dad wrote in his journal, "Music from a stringed instrument is a result of tension. Help me to trust the music you are making in my life." Suffering results in living music that brings glory to God.

Joseph did not erase his memory, but God helped him to transform it. Joseph went through immense suffering when he was sold into slavery by his own brothers. He endured injustice from a wrongful accusation from Potiphar's wife. He continued to prosper in prison and interpreted dreams for the baker and cupbearer; but the cupbearer, upon his good fortune, "did not remember Joseph, but forgot him" (Gen. 40:23). After two more years in prison, Joseph had every reason to despair and lose hope; and yet God did not forget Him, and Joseph did not forget that God remembered Him. Later, when he was lifted up to the second-highest position in Egypt, Joseph named his firstborn Manasseh, which means "God has made me forget all my trouble and all my father's household" (Gen. 41:51).

Does this mean that Joseph's memory was erased from the pain of the past? No, rather God transformed his memory so that he no longer dwelt on the negative effects of the suffering by the hands of men but rather on the provision by the hand of God. Joseph revealed this memory transformation when he exclaimed to his brothers, "As for you, you meant evil against me, but God meant it for good in order to bring about the present result, to preserve many people alive" (Gen. 50:20). Joseph still remembered the evil by his brothers but now placed it in proper context—the hand of God's salvation. "For the LORD takes pleasure in His people; He will beautify the afflicted ones with salvation" (Ps. 149:4). "Remember this, had any other condition been better for you than the one in which you are, divine love would have placed you there."[7]

Suffering results from living in a fallen and evil world. The wonder of God is not how He uses goodness for your good, but how He uses evil for your good. As an example from creation, certain types of figs require a special breed of wasp for pollination. The female wasp crawls inside the narrow hole at the bottom of the fig. The hole narrows so that the wasp cannot back out, and she

7 Charles H. Spurgeon, *Morning and Evening Daily Readings,* Web. 15 October, 2020, monergism.com.

loses her wings and dies. If she dies in a female fig, she pollinates the fig so that it goes on to produce edible fruit. Before you decide if you will ever eat a fig again, the female fig also produces an enzyme that completely digests the wasp.[8] Similarly, God uses evil to produce fruit in your life, a mystery that only God understands. You must trust God where you cannot trace Him.[9] This concept of goodness in suffering extends right to the foot of the cross. Memory brings to mind not just the triumph of the resurrection but also the suffering of the cross. The suffering of the cross is not erased but rather remembered rightly for what it accomplished—victory.

Remember your roots

Similarly, the next part of the "remember recipe" involves your roots. Christians must remember where they came from—a helpless and hopeless state. Similar to the call to Israel to "remember that you were a slave in the land of Egypt" (Deut. 5:15), the Christian must remember that "you were dead in your trespasses and sins, in which you formerly walked" (Eph. 2:1–2). These roots underpin worship, a glorious response to rescue and redemption. The appreciation for the grandness of redemption requires an appreciation for the depth of the helplessness. The temptation of the prideful mind is to minimize the past redemption, the depth of the need, and the grandness of the rescue. You distort memory to think better of self and less of God's grace. Man is the chief of creatures but is also the chief of sinners.[10] The chief of sinners needed the friend of sinners, Jesus Christ, to pay the price.

Remember your salvation

Remember your salvation. Salvation is a crucial part of remembrance, not to be pushed aside once it is obtained but constantly brought back to mind. Salvation is not just a one-time past event

8 Luis Villazon, "Is it true there are dead wasps in figs?", Web. 11 September, 2020, sciencefocus.com.

9 Charles H. Spurgeon, "The Happy Christian," 1867, accessed 19 July, 2021, spurgeon.org.

10 G. K. Chesterton, *Orthodoxy*, (Moody Publishers, 2009), 142.

but a present reality that infuses into everyday life and thinking. Salvation ensures your position as an adopted and redeemed son. Peter knew the central importance of salvation in memory as he "will always be ready to remind you these things, even though you already know them" (2 Peter 1:12). What things? He is referring back to "the precious promises" (2 Peter 1:4) that are yours when you are saved. Your salvation does not arrive at your doorstep like a solitary, single package but rather bursts forth in immeasurable inheritance that lasts forever. Salvation is applied continually, and memory must work to remember it constantly.

Remember not just the theology of salvation but also your personal story of salvation, even if you think it is ordinary. Yes, your story might be extraordinary like that of Saul on the road to Damascus; but for many other readers, your story might sound more like that of Lydia who listened to the gospel, and "the Lord opened her heart to respond to the things spoken by Paul" (Acts 16:14). Lydia and Paul's stories vary in context and circumstances; but the true miracle is the same: God intervened and saved sinners by His amazing grace. You were dead *in* sin and now dead *to* sin. Remember your redemption, captured in the simple swap of a preposition.

REMEMBER OTHERS

History, a compilation of the memories, reminds of past failures and triumphs. The challenges of historical analysis is that those in the present lack the full comprehension of the context of the past and might be missing important facts. Criticism of others' history is much easier than the creation of your own history. Care needs to be taken to not discard history but learn from both failures and triumphs.

The history of the family

The age of the Internet sadly necessitates the argument for the value of generational memory, the passing down of knowledge and experience from the older to the younger. The younger now turn to Google instead of to Grandma for wisdom; but Google is not Grandma. Google is simply a search engine without feelings, while a grandma is a caring soul with context. Not everyone is blessed with Christian parents, grandparents, and great-grandparents. You might be the first Christian in your family tree, but God clearly states the benefits of a godly heritage, which might need to start with you. Memory forms a bridge between generations to allow for the passage of knowledge and wisdom from the past to the present. If this memory bridge is missing in your family tree, turn to the church and community memory.

The history of the church family

On a global scale, when you became a Christian and part of the family of God, you inherited the history of the church with all its triumphs and failures, the reformation alongside the religious wars, the creeds and the conflicts. This family is your family. The church family provides identity and a common thread that unites in conflict but also gives opportunity to learn and grow from the past. These same concepts apply to the local church community. The local community must pass along a full history. Without history, the local community does not just lose identity but also loses the foundation of maturity and growth accumulated over the years, and is liable to repeat the same mistakes of the past. A forgotten past guarantees future regression. Why? "That which has been is that which will be, and that which has been done is that which will be done. So there is nothing new under the sun" (Eccl. 1:9). A community mistake, then, is not a new failure but a repeated failure from unlearned history.

The history of failures

God recorded failures in the Bible for a reason. 1 Corinthians 10 reminds the church of the sins of Israel "as examples for us, so that we would not crave evil things as they also craved" (1 Cor. 10:6). Paul then recounted the sins of idolatry, immorality, and grumbling committed by Israel. These things "were written for our instruction" (1 Cor. 10:11). Why do we need to be reminded of these examples? Because these pitfalls are not just ancient Middle East snares but present deceptions. Israel was given all the blessings and assistance to succeed but did not please God. Christians today need to be careful to guard against the mindset that they are above these old snares.

Remember Israel's history as a means to humility. "Therefore let him who thinks he stand take heed that he does not fall" (1 Cor. 10:12). History reminds that no one is too tall to fall. Remember biblical history to also learn that God is faithful "who will not allow you to be tempted beyond what you are able, but with the temptation will provide the way of escape also, so that you will be able to endure it" (1 Cor. 10:13). God provided a way forward for Israel in each of these failures. History, then, not only brings humble sobriety but also hopeful steadfastness.

So what are you to do when you fail? In *The Pilgrim's Progress*, Hopeful and Christian escaped the dungeon of Giant Despair. When they arrived back at the place where they had hopped over the fence and left the road, they discussed how to warn future pilgrims who would come the same way. They did not want others to make the same mistake and wander onto the giant's property, so they built a pillar and engraved it with this message: "Over the stile is the way to Doubting Castle, which is kept by Giant Despair, who despises the King of the Celestial Country, and seeks to destroy holy pilgrims."[11] Because of this sign, Bunyan noted many future pilgrims escaped the despair that awaited them at the castle. Christian and Hopeful did not hide their mistake but warned future generations. Instead of keeping silent for fear of embarrassment, they used the failure for personal growth and to teach others. Failure is a failure if no one learns from it. Bunyan, who struggled with doubt and despair, wrote his own warning to future pilgrims; the pillar is called *The Pilgrim's Progress*.

---

11 John Bunyan, *The Pilgrim's Progress* (London: Gall and Inglis, undated), 156.

The history of triumphs

The Bible records not only failures but also triumphs. Men and women fill the pages of the Bible with heroic acts of faith. The biblical narrative includes biographies of men and women whom you are called to imitate—a great cloud of witnesses. The writer of Hebrews commands the readers to "Remember those who led you, who spoke the word of God to you; and considering the result of their conduct, imitate their faith" (Heb. 13:7). Hebrews 11 serves as the biblical collection of biographical recaps—reminders of Old Testament saints who endured as they trusted that God would keep His covenant promises. These men and women in the hall of faith pleased God as they believed that God would reward "those who seek Him" (Heb. 11:6).

The benefits of biblical and extrabiblical Christian biography are numerous. John Piper commented, "Biographies have served as much as any other human force in my life to resist the inertia of mediocrity. Without them I tend to forget what joy is in relentless God-besotted labor and aspiration."[12] When you read about men and women who persevered, the perseverance rubs off on you and gives you the energy to continue on.

The abridged narrative

Hebrews 11 is striking, not just for what is mentioned—the acts of faith—but what is not mentioned: the failures. As you peruse the hall of faith, no mention is made of Noah's drunkenness, Abraham's lying, Sarah's scoffing, Isaac's trickery, Jacob's deception, Joseph's pride, Moses' anger, and the list goes on and on. Instead, the writer emphasizes the triumphs of these flawed heroes. To widen the lens, the New Testament writers follow this pattern of highlighting faith and not mentioning failure, to such a degree that the New Testament is almost completely silent in regard to Old Testament saints' failures. The examples of failure the New Testament writers use include those who were not saints, like Cain (1 John 3:12), Balaam (2 Peter 2:15–16), and Lot's wife (Luke17:32). As al-

12 John Piper, *Brothers, We are not Professionals* (Broadman & Holman Publishers. 2002), 90.

ready mentioned, New Testament writers use the failures of Israel to learn from, but not the failures of individual saints who trusted in God.

The dual narrative

The Old Testament writers, though, provide the narrative that includes these failures. In fact, the Old Testament rarely narrates an Old Testament saint without including failures. Excluding the prophets like Daniel and Jeremiah, the only story of an Old Testament saint without a mentioned failure is Abel. Enoch might be included here, but his story is limited to genealogy and a single statement that "he walked with God" (Gen. 5:22). Even though failures are not mentioned in their brief biographies, the reader knows that Abel and Enoch sinned (Rom. 3:23).

The Bible, then, contains two narratives. The Old Testament emphasizes an unabridged narrative that includes the failures, while the New Testament narrative emphasizes an abridged narrative that highlights the triumphs of faith of the Old Testament saints.

How are these flawed Old Testament characters remembered in Hebrews 11 for their faith? The answer sits in the bracketed context. First, the writer of Hebrews notes that "for by one offering He (Christ) has perfected for all time those who are sanctified" (Heb. 10:14). The writer reminds them of the New Covenant that "their sins and their lawless deeds, I will remember no more." The New Testament writers focus on faith and not failure, and in a way, demonstrate how God the Father views His children through the blood of Christ. Through Christ's blood, God "forgets" the failure and only "remembers" the faith. The New Testament abridged narrative is made possible by Christ who perfects your faith.

Hebrews 12 encourages the encumbered and entangled Christian to fix his eyes on Jesus, "the author and perfecter of faith, who for the joy set before Him endured the cross, despising the shame, and has sat down at the right hand of the throne of God" (Heb. 12:2). Jesus perfects faith such that the failures are forgotten, and the faith is forged in memory. The failures of the heroes pointed ahead to the need for a perfect hero to come and rescue. Christ succeeded where all others failed. He succeeded not just in personal perfection but in a sacrifice that applied that perfection to those who believe. Through His work on the cross and victory over the grave, the sinner no longer is labelled by his sin. The murderer is no longer known as a murderer; the liar is no longer known as a liar. This is not hagiography, the idealizing of the saints. The sins and failures were not excused; rather they were covered and removed.

The Bible provides this personal balance in the dual narrative—the Old Testament narrative that includes failures, and the New Testament narrative that highlights faith. The Christian must look at the dual narrative and find balance. The unabridged narrative of Old Testament heroes with failures reminds you of your failures. These heroes are like you and me. As you bring to mind your own unabridged narrative with your failures, the remembrance brings humility and also hope, hope that God used these flawed heroes and can use you too.[13] As you then recount the abridged New Testament narrative of Old Testament heroes and their remarkable faith, you are also reminded of your small faith authored and perfected by Christ. This abridged narrative inspires praise and worship for the fruit of faith.

Off the Atlantic coast of Central and South America, the four-eyed fish swims. The fish actually has two eyes, but each eye is divided into two halves by a strip of tissue. Each eye has two pupils and two corneas. The upper eye is sensitive to green-light wavelengths of the air while the lower eye is sensitive to yellow-light wavelengths of the muddy waters. The fish swims on the surface of the water so that the upper eye sees above for predators, while the lower eye sees below for food.[14] You must have two sets of eyes, "one to see imperfections in ourselves, the other to see what is good."[15] This dual narrative gives the Christian a balanced perspective, both to look at your full life with its failures but also to look through eyes that focus on Christ's work that perfects faith. This balance protects from the predator of pride and feeds the soul with grace.

13 John Piper, "Thanksgiving for the lives of flawed saints," 18 November, 1999, Web. 11 September, 2020, desiringgod.org.

14 Jonathan Balcombe, *What a Fish Knows,* Scientific American (2017), 28.

15 Richard Sibbes, *The Bruised Reed* (Edinburgh: The Banner of Truth Trust 1998), 35.

The way the Bible remembers others teaches you how to view your own personal history. Survey these heroes and observe that "Christ refuses none for weakness of parts, that none should be discouraged, but accepts none for greatness, that none should be lifted up with that which is of little reckoning with God."[16] Run the race with a memory of the personal past but with eyes fixed forward toward Christ.

REMEMBER THE BIBLE

The final object of the command to remember in the Bible is the Bible. This command is not conceited but rather an acknowledgement of the importance of the truth of God's Word. If God's Word is the most precious source of truth, it must be most accessible in memory. Anthony Burgess writes,

> What a precious and excellent memory is that which is like a mine of gold, or an Apothecary's shop that can from the Scripture presently fetch what antidotes against sin, or cordials to revive that he pleaseth? And truly our memory should be filled up only with Scripture considerations. This is the cabinet and choice closet of thy soul. If a man should take his cabinet that was for jewels and precious stones, and fill it only with mud and dirt, would it not be exceeding great folly?"[17]

The answer to the question is a resounding yes! Fill up the cabinets of memory with the jewels of Scripture. Moses emphasized this importance in his charge to Joshua to remember God's law so that "the book of the Law shall not depart from your mouth" (Josh. 1:8) The memory cabinet of God's Word includes God's law as a reminder of the unattainable perfect standard but also includes God's covenants.

"Remember His covenant forever" (1 Chron 16:14a). Remembering God's covenant requires a memory of the past, present, and future. Abraham remembered the past covenant promise of Isaac, acted in the present to offer Isaac in faith,

16 Ibid., 23.

17 Anthony Burgess, *The Extent of Original Sin in Every Faculty of the Soul,* Web. 24 March 2021, monergism.com, 90.

and expected in the future that God would be able to raise Isaac from the dead (Heb. 11:19). The remembrance of the covenant promises drives faith that flourishes in any season.

The Bible is a road map, necessary for survival. Life constantly shifts like the tides of the ocean. The three-inch frillfin goby swims over tide pools at high tide, memorizing the depressions in the rocks that will form future tide pools at low tide. The fish creates a mental topographical map of the tide pool during the "good" times, when the water is plentiful, to be, in anticipation of the "bad" times, when the water is low. As the water recedes, these torpedo-shaped fish leap from tide pool to tide pool to escape to safety 97 percent of the time. Without such high-tide experience to map the area, their success dropped to 15 percent.[18] Similarly, the memorization of the topography of the Bible in high times is necessary for successful use in the low times. A disregard for the Word disarms the Christian.

Summary

The Bible commands you to remember God, you, others, and the Bible. Why are these worth remembering? Because each is eternal: God, the souls of you and me, and God's Word. God commands you to invest in what is lasting.

FORGET THE UNIMPORTANT

Remembrance is commonly celebrated as a virtue, while forgetfulness is loathed as the foe. However, proper forgetfulness in many ways is a friend. Consider what life would be like without forgetfulness. Dr. Luria wrote about a Russian named Shereshevskin who possessed superior autobiographical memory. Besides documenting the amazing feats of memory, Luria also captured the frustrations that accompanied the inability to forget. Shereshevskin needed to learn how to forget, to erase images he no longer needed or wanted.[19] Forgetfulness reduces clutter

18 L. R. Aronson, "Further studies on orientation and jumping behavior in the gobiid fish, bathygobius soporator," *Annals of the New York Academy of Sciences* vol. 188 (1971), 378–92.

19 A. R. Luria, *The Mind of a Mnemonist* (Basic Books Inc. 1968), 68–69.

in the past and allows for clarity in the present. "It seems like you hold onto everything, and it seems like you're just stuck in the past all the time."[20] The vivid detailed past actively scrolls in the present as you try to write on a page already covered with words.

In God's infinite wisdom, He commands you not just to remember but also to forget. Here, forgetfulness does not mean a complete inability to recall ever again. Rather, forgetfulness carries the idea that you may recall in fact but without affect. In other words, you are not dwelling on the object to the point that you are weighed down and enslaved by it.

Forget past accolades

To evaluate the call to forgetfulness, Paul writes, "Forgetting what lies behind and straining forward to what lies ahead, I press on toward the goal for the prize of the upward call of God in Christ Jesus" (Phil. 3:13b–14). In this context, Paul describes his religious credentials, including his ethnicity, religious fervor, and Pharisaical righteousness. On the road to Damascus, Paul encountered the resurrected Christ; and all these religious accolades evaporated in the shining light of his Savior. With Paul's transformation, he no longer looked to the past and his own "righteousness" but now looked to Christ and His righteousness.

"Forgetting what lies behind" equates to forgetting self. Self-adoration leads to self-attack. If you stare in the mirror long enough, vanity destroys like a beta-fish that attacks its own image in a mirror until it dies. The beta thinks another enemy is in the water, but the only enemy in the water is you. So pray with the psalmist to "turn my eyes away from looking at vanity, and revive me in Your ways" (Ps. 119:37).

Forget the past way of life

In salvation, you not only leave behind past "righteousness" but also past "unrighteousness." The transformation beckons you forward in the race and to "not turn back to the weak and worthless elemental things" (Gal. 4:9) that formerly enslaved you. When

20 Alex Spiegel, "When Memories Never Fade, the Past Can Poison the Present." 27 December, 2013, Web. 25 March, 2021, npr.org.

you are made alive in Christ, you "consider the members of your earthly body as dead to immorality, impurity, passion, evil desire, and greed, which amounts to idolatry" (Col. 3:5). Despite a transformation, the battle rages as the worthless things beckon you to return to the wasteland.

In medical school, a young girl came in to the pediatrician's office for a fever for five days accompanied by joint pains and a bumpy rash first seen on her hands. No one could figure out the cause, despite many tests. Then, one question solved the mystery. "Do you have any pets?" Yes, she had a pet rat, and the pet rat liked to kiss her on the lips. These symptoms fit rat-bite fever, a serious condition that kills one in eight patients. The cure was simple—penicillin, the first antibiotic discovered. Despite almost dying, the girl kept the pet rat. The source of illness remained close by, right next to her in her room.

In a way similar to the young girl, instead of removing former sins far away, you keep the rat dangerously close. Instead of forgetting the "unrighteous" past, you place reminders that entangle the present. The idols of the past sparkle in the light of the bedside lamp.

Forget past offenses

Forgive and forget. These two words share the first three letters, "for," but the endings of "give" and "get" emphasize the challenge to combine their actions. Is it truly possible to forgive and forget? Yes, if you carefully define forgetfulness to mean that an offense may still be recalled in fact but without bitter effect. Forgiveness does not mean the past offense is condoned or justified. Forgiveness is not permissiveness. Rather, forgiveness acknowledges the pain as pain but extinguishes the bitterness in the pain.

In forgiveness, the type of offenses may range widely from a verbal argument to violent assault; the degree of hurt will also appropriately range widely. The principles discussed here do not attempt to dive into these complexities but rather give broad overarching principles.

Overall, distorted memory minimizes your own offenses against others and magnifies others' offenses against you.

"People remember what has already taken place differently. And they disagree about how to move forward."[21] Distorted remembrance demands a distorted path to forgiveness. Even if you are right and blameless in that particular argument, distorted memory blinds you to your own past offenses against others. You enter and exit each argument as the one offended and never the offender. Solomon provides insight here: "Also, do not take seriously all words which are spoken, so that you will not hear your servant cursing you. For you also have realized that you likewise have many times cursed others" (Eccl. 7:21–22). Forgetfulness in forgiveness begins with remembering your own need for forgiveness.

The way to forgiveness is through a greater remembrance—remembrance of Christ's forgiveness of you. Christ realigns memory. By remembering your own offenses against God paid on the cross, forgiveness may be extended to others. Paul connects God's forgiveness and your forgiveness when he writes, "Be kind to one another, tenderhearted, forgiving one another, as God in Christ forgave you" (Eph. 4:32). Remember God's forgiveness of your offenses to "forget" others' offenses toward you. The offense is no longer bathed in bitterness but blood—blood that pardoned your sin. The one who is forgiven much forgives much; the one who is forgiven little forgives little (Luke 7:47).

Forgiveness is a miracle that God extends to you, and forgiveness is a miracle that you extend to others. The miracle takes place in the heart. The zebra fish provides as an amazing example of a miracle of the heart. Research led by Dr. Wang induced heart attacks in zebra fish that destroyed up to sixty percent of the heart muscle, but these fish possess an amazing ability to regenerate the heart muscle and restore function within several days.[22] Unfortunately, when the human heart is damaged by a heart attack, the heart cannot grow new muscle. The damage is permanent. But when the spiritual heart is injured, God

21 Chris Braun, *Unpacking Forgiveness: Biblical Answers for Complex Questions and Deep Wounds* (Wheaton, IL: Crossway, 2008), 179.

22 Jinhu Wang, et al., "The regenerative capacity of zebrafish reverses cardiac failure caused by genetic cardiomyocyte depletion," *Development* 15 August, 2011, 138 (16): 3421–30.

regenerates your heart and gives you the capacity to fully forgive (Ezek. 36:26–27).

In my life, forgiveness was tested in my family's fatal car accident. Eyewitnesses reported that a black pickup truck cut in front of my family's car. My sister veered to avoid the truck and went across the grassy median to collide head-on with a semitruck. My dad, mom, and sisters died instantly; the driver of the black truck continued down the freeway. The night of the accident, I prayed to God to keep me from anger. The Lord answered. I write this account without anger, remembering the pain but forgetting the bitterness. Forgiveness is like the dawn when the sunlight peeks out in the morning. The stars, bright against the velvet black of night, fade away in the sunlight. The stars might be invisible, but they are still present. The Son of God shines His forgiveness upon you and the bitterness of the offenses of others fades away. Forgiveness is not really forgetfulness but rather right remembrance.

Summary

Purposeful forgetfulness declutters memory. With forgetfulness of the unimportant, memory concentrates on the important. The unimportant include vanity, idolatry, and others' offenses against you. The unimportant all share the same characteristic: transience. What is eternal ought to be remembered while what fades ought to be forgotten.

The ROYGBIV acronym coincides with the colors of the rainbow: red, orange, yellow, green, blue, indigo, and violet. It will now serve to help us remember the commands of memory. Remember Others, You, God, the Bible and forget Idolatry and Vanity. Don't forget that the commands are empowered by His promises (the rainbow).

HOW TO REMEMBER
HIS COMMANDS AND PROMISES

These commands need to be remembered. God provides tools and cues to assist your memory, but effort is required.

Scripture memory
....

Memorize verses and passages that you value. "A crucial factor in deciding whether something will be learned and remembered is its meaningfulness to the learner."[23] Why memorize? David answers, "I have stored up Your word in my heart, that I might not sin against You" (Ps. 119:11). Scripture that is buried in the heart produces holiness, vital for life.

The Clark's Nutcracker, a bird that lives in the Rocky Mountains, gathers more than thirty thousand pine seeds in a summer, with the utilization of a special pouch under the tongue to carry about one hundred seeds at a time.[24] These seeds get deposited in about five thousand secret caches around a hundred square miles. Despite the small size of this bird's brain, the Clark's Nutcracker will locate around seventy percent of these stores in the winter, despite the seasonal changes of the terrain.[25] This bird is known to dig down under snow and rocks with precision to find its buried food treasure, crucial for survival. In a similar way, bury the Word in your heart to be drawn upon in the winter, food for a bleak season, words to be eaten (Jer. 15:16). The internalization of the Word sets Christians apart. "The worldling has his treasure in jewels without him; the Christian has them within him."[26] By internalizing the treasure, the treasure is protected from the elements and cannot corrode. This stored-up treasure preserves life.

---

23 Alan Baddeley, *Essentials of Human Memory* (Psychology Press, 2014), 78.

24 Jennifer Ackerman, *The Genius of Birds* (Penguin Books, 2017), 211.

25 Ibid.

26 William Cowper, "Psalm 119," in *The Treasury of David,* vol. 2, (Thomas Nelson Publishers, 1984), 165.

Meditation

·················

By implication, memorization of Scripture goes beyond reading and rote recollection to meditation. Meditation moves Scripture from the intellect into the affections. John Wells noted, "The memory is the chest to lay up a truth, but meditation is the palate to feed upon it. There is as much difference between a truth remembered and a truth meditated as between a cordial in the glass and a cordial drunk down."[27] Words move from the intellect of the mind into the bowels, the seat of the affections. Memory should not just sample but savor.

Thomas Watson spoke in 1676 at the funeral for this very same pastor, John Wells, on the shortness of time. In that speech, Watson asked the question, "How should we improve this short time?"[28] His answer—meditation. On the surface, meditation appears to be a waste of time; what, you might ask, are you truly accomplishing in pondering? And yet this is the way to closer communion with God. "Meditation cements divine truths into the mind. It brings God and the soul together. Meditation is the bellows of the affections. It gives a sight and a taste of invisible glory."[29] Meditation integrates words about God into affections for God; words of the mind into words of the soul.

What you meditate upon shapes what you look like. While in emergency medicine residency training, I remember a patient who checked into the ER for concern about his skin. He told me that his skin was turning a yellow-orange color. He showed me the palms of his hands, which were yellow especially in the creases. Immediately, I was concerned about jaundice and liver failure. I sent the standard labs and went to chart; but something did not fit. His eyes were not yellow, a common manifestation of jaundice from liver problems. Heading back to the room, I asked the man one question that solved the mystery. What is your diet like? He told me he ate carrots—lots of carrots. He was a day laborer for a carrot farmer and was paid in carrots. He could not afford to eat much else. Carotonemia, yellow skin from eating a large amount

27 John Wells, "Psalm 63," in *The Treasury of David,* vol. 1 (Thomas Nelson Publishers, 1984), 76.

28 Thomas Watson, "Time's Shortness," accessed 21 April, 2021, gracegems.org.

29 Ibid.

of foods rich in carotene like carrots, was not dangerous to him but did change his appearance.

In a similar way, when you consume and meditate upon the Word of God, it changes your appearance. You begin to look like what you "eat." Your skin does not turn yellow-orange like a carrot but rather your life produces good fruit. The psalmist captures this imagery when he writes, "His delight is in the law of the LORD, and on His law he meditates day and night. He is like a tree planted by streams of water that yields its fruit in its season" (Ps. 1:2–3a). The one who meditates on the Lord produces fruit.

Chapter 7
Application Questions

1. Why is it important to remember not just the commands but also the promises of God?

2. What is the role of memory in suffering? Why is there a place to remember suffering and not just erase it? How does the cross inform your view on suffering?

3. Remember your own personal story of salvation and write down the details. How does your story incorporate the steps of the Gospel? Why is it important to remember your "roots?"

4. What is the dual narrative of Old Testament saints? How do both the abridged and unabridged narratives affect you? Which narrative do you tend to neglect the most?

5. What things are Christians called to forget? What are the benefits of forgetfulness?

6. How is meditation different than memorization? What hinders your meditation?

8

The Fruit of Redemptive Memory

Remembering in the Bible results in fruit—an active process. The action of redemptive memory transforms you more and more to look like Christ. The believer remembers the commands and promises of God, and this remembrance does not simply pass through, but settles in and sanctifies you. "Therefore, having these promises, beloved, let us cleanse ourselves from all defilement of flesh and spirit, perfecting holiness in the fear of God" (2 Cor. 7:1). The remembrance of God's promises cleanses you into His holy likeness for the purpose of bringing Him glory.

Sanctification colors in the lines of God's attributes. You can say God is faithful, but how much more rich and full to reflect back on a life lived with the color of God's faithfulness now visible. The adjectives to describe God move from words with plain definition to words with vibrant color and story. This fruit-producing transformation of the mind is captured best by Paul when he writes, "Do not be conformed to this world but be transformed by the renewing of your mind, so that you may prove what the will of God is, that which is good and acceptable and perfect" (Rom. 12:2).

The active practice of right remembrance (sanctification) results from a right relationship with God (justification). Notice your position in Christ: "Therefore if you have been raised up with Christ, keep seeking the things above, where Christ is, seated at the right hand of God" (Col. 3:1). This elevated and raised position arises from your adoption as a son and daughter by the Father. The Father graciously gives you a seat at His table.

In my childhood house, no room better captured relationship like the dining room. As a member of the family, each person had a seat at the dining room table, a space to sit, eat, and share life. The table served as a centerpiece for conversation, for sitting and lingering. My dad built our wood-stained table with two benches and two leaves that could be added for guests. After the car accident, the table now sits in my house as a centerpiece for meals, crafts, and birthday parties. The same spots that occupied my dad, mom, and sisters are now filled by my wife and our three children. The tabletop stain has worn off from so much use over the years. The table leaves have been pulled in and out countless times as guests from all around the world have eaten at this table. When guests sit down and eat, they are sitting in those same spots and are treated like family.

The Father gives seats at the table to His children but, beyond that, gives all the rights and privileges of family. You are not a guest but a family member. With this new family identity, the practice follows to "[s]et your mind on the things above, not on the things that are on earth" (Col. 3:2). As Christ is at the center of your new identity, you become transformed into "the image of the One who created him—a renewal in which there is no distinction between Greek and Jew, circumcised and uncircumcised, barbarian, Scythian, slave and freeman, but Christ is all, and in all" (Col. 3:10b–11). Christ who created you in His image now transforms you into His image.

This transformation of the mind reaches to great heights as Paul states, "For who has known the mind of the Lord, that he will instruct Him? But, we have the mind of Christ" (1 Cor. 2:16). The mind of man is illuminated to understand the truth through the Holy Spirit, in such a way that you have the mind of Christ! This does not mean that you will know and understand everything.

Rather, you have a mind now receptive to the truth and able to recall the truth. Your mind is capable of joyful delight in the Savior, no longer dismissive and even hostile toward spiritual things.

Take a moment to imagine what your life would be like without any memory of Christ—His goodness, mercy, lovingkindness, presence in your life. What emptiness, loneliness, and darkness! This is why Isaiah exclaims, "O LORD, we have waited for You eagerly; Your name, even Your memory, is the desire of our souls" (Isa. 26:8b). This desire for God overflows into the fruit of redeemed memory both in attitude and action.

HUMILITY

The first fruit of a redeemed memory is humility. Humility is positional, born out of a right understanding of the placement of self in relation to God. Self gives up center stage in the mind. Paul implores the Corinthians to remember their calling, that God chose the foolish, lowly, and despised "so that no human being might boast in the presence of God" (1 Cor. 1:29b). The free gift and unearned grace of the gospel subjugates the desire for human superiority. Paul again addresses the church in Corinth: "For who regards you as superior? What do you have that you did not receive? And if you did receive it, why do you boast as if you had not received it (1 Cor. 4:7)?" The gospel removes the perpetual thinking on self and replaces it with humility, a thinking on self less.[1]

So what enthralls the mind to produce forgetfulness of self? God—His beauty and magnificence. The memory returns to its original and primary purpose: to glorify and worship God, the One who is superior in every way. Martyn Lloyd-Jones identified self as the greatest enemy, and the only way to battle is to "be so absorbed in what you are doing and in the realization of the presence of God ... that you forget yourself completely."[2] Redeemed remembrance is actually a right forgetfulness, a forgetfulness of self.

1 Tim Keller, *The Freedom of Self-Forgetfulness* (10Publishing, 2012), 32.

2 D. Martyn Lloyd-Jones, *Preaching and Preachers* (Zondervan Publishing House, 1971), 264.

COMFORT

In Suffering
....

From this position of humility, the redeemed memory supplies comfort to the present, especially in the midst of suffering. A person may find refuge in the painful present by remembering the past. Asaph gives a template to follow in Psalm 77. He cries to God in the day of trouble. His "soul refused to be comforted" (Ps. 77:2). The psalmist raises questions about God and His character. Is God truly who He says He is? "Has His lovingkindness ceased forever? Has His promise come to an end? Has God forgotten to be gracious or has He in anger withdrawn His compassion? Then I said, 'It is my grief, that the right hand of the Most High has changed'" (Ps 77:7–10). Here is the fork in the road where doubt rises up and questions the character of God.

The psalmist answers these doubts: "Remember the deeds of the LORD; surely I will remember Your wonders of old" (Ps. 77:11). Commenting on this passage, Spurgeon says, "If no good was in the present, memory ransacked the past to find consolation. She fain would borrow a light from the altars of yesterday to light the gloom of today."[3] The psalmist meditated on the Exodus, the salvation of God's people. He relived the Exodus with the waters fleeing, the rain pouring, the thunder roaring, the lightning flashing, and the earth trembling (Ps. 77:16–20). He remembered and reenacted God leading the people, and he found comfort. Today, believers need to go back to salvation at the cross while in the midst of suffering. Do not yield to despair. Even when Calvary appears like a speck, ask Him to carry you back to the foot of the cross. Remember that Christ sympathizes as He Himself unjustly suffered and was acquainted with much grief. Remember Christ saved you from the pit of eternal destruction; surely He can sustain you in present trouble.

Notice comfort is not provided by memory through forgetfulness but right remembrance. Comfort is not forgetting the problems, like they do not exist, but remembering the promises of the Comforter. As my dad wrote in his journal, "A

3 Charles H. Spurgeon, "Psalm 77," in *The Treasury of David*, vol. 1, (Thomas Nelson Publishers, 1984), 313.

good day is not when I forget my problems but rather cast them on You." Comfort is attainable even when circumstances remain unchanged because the Source of the comfort is greater than the circumstances. God implements a variety of mercies for a variety of miseries. Cast your bucket of misery into the sea of God's mercies and watch Him swallow them up.[4] For the Christian, misery has limits while mercy is limitless, because misery is bound by time on earth while mercy extends to eternity in heaven.

In Grief

God cares about your grief, but He does not remove all sadness. Sadness in grief is not a sickness that needs a cure or sinfulness that needs a confession. Grief properly recognizes that death is a disorder of a broken earth, unnatural, out of sync with the original design. Death amputates. In speaking of the death of his wife, C.S. Lewis writes,

> To say the patient is getting over it after an operation for appendicitis is one thing; after he's had his leg cut off is quite another. After that operation, either the wounded stump heals, or the man dies. If it heals, the fierce, continuous pain will stop. Presently he'll get back his strength and be able to stump about on his wooden leg. He has "got over it." But he will probably have recurrent pains in the stump all his life, and perhaps pretty bad ones; and he will always be a one-legged man. There will be hardly any moment when he forgets it. Bathing, dressing, sitting down and getting up again, even lying in bed will all be different. His whole way of life will be changed.[5]

C. S. Lewis accurately summarizes the death of a loved one as a limb that will never grow back. So how does memory bring comfort in the midst of loss?

Thomas Watson answers, "True religion does not *banish*

---

4 Jeremiah Burroughs, *The Rare Jewel of Christian Contentment* (CreatedSpace Independent Publishing, 2013), 125.

5 C. S. Lewis, *A Grief Observed* (Harper-Collins e-books. 2009), 52–53.

grief, it *bounds* it."[6] Grace puts a lower limit on the depths of grief. "There is a bottom to the profoundest of our misery. Our winters shall not frown forever: summer shall too smile."[7] Tulips demonstrate how winter's frown turns into spring's smile. A tulip bulb requires cold temperatures in the winter for about twelve weeks. The bulbs might appear inactive in the cold, but a lot is happening underground. An important enzyme called alpha amylase works to break down stores of starches into sugar.[8] The sugar water can withstand colder temperatures, which promote sugar transport from storage into the growing bud. As spring approaches and the temperature begins to rise, the sugar now serves as energy for the bulb to grow a stalk and bloom with a smile. So often, God uses the cold of winter to cause you to grow in amazing ways. Memory feasts on the sugars of past grace for comfort in the present—a remembrance of the previous winter and the vibrant spring that followed.

The Bible speaks to the abounding grace that God supplies in times of need. Like a shepherd, God binds up the broken limb of His lamb and carries the lamb on His shoulders (Isa. 40:11). During times of brokenness, He carries you close and near as you heal. His grace is sufficient in times of weakness (2 Cor. 12:9).

In an earlier chapter, Naomi served as an example of bitterness. But the story of Naomi did not end there. Naomi experienced the deaths of her husband and two sons, and responded in bitterness. Yet, Naomi was not empty-handed as she claimed; God had given her Ruth, a gift of grace. After Boaz and Ruth met by divine appointment and married, Ruth bore a son. God was glorified when the townswomen said to Naomi, "'May he also be to you a restorer of life and a sustainer of your old age; for your daughter-in-law, who loves you and is better to you than seven sons, has given birth to him.' Then Naomi took the child and laid him in her lap, and became his nurse. The neighbor women gave him a name, saying, 'A son has been born to Naomi!' So they named

6 Thomas Watson, "Time's Shortness," accessed 21 April, 2021, gracegems.org.

7 Charles H. Spurgeon, *Gleanings among the Sheaves* (New York: Fleming B. Revell, 1869), 13.

8 H. Lambrechts, et al, "Carbohydrate Status of Tulip Bulbs during Cold-Induced Flower Stalk Elongation and Flowering," *Plant physiology* vol. 104,2 (1994), 515–20.

him Obed. He is the father of Jesse, the father of David." (See Ruth 4:13–17.) God's grace comforted Naomi through Ruth and then restored her joy. When grief is overwhelming, find comfort in the remembrance of the biblical narratives of redemption like Naomi and cling to the promises of His grace.

In conclusion, a song, *He Giveth More Grace* came to mind. My dad used to sing it to me at night when I would struggle to get to sleep, kept up by the cares of the world.

> *He giveth more grace when the burdens grow greater.*
> *He sendeth more strength when the labors increase.*
> *To added affliction, He addeth His mercy.*
> *To multiplied trials, His multiplied peace.*[9]

HOPE

Comfort rests in the present, while hope looks to the future. Present comfort and future hope mingle. David juxtaposes them when he writes, "Remember Your word to your servant, in which You have made me *hope*. This is my *comfort* in my affliction, that Your promise gives me life" (Ps. 119:49–50, emphasis added). Comfort and hope sit side by side in the text but also sit side by side in life.

Jeremiah highlights the relationship between hope and memory in one of my favorite memory passages, Lamentations 3. Here, the author cries out to the Lord on account of the destruction of Jerusalem for her sin. The poet grieves the devastation on a personal and communal level. In despair, he writes these words: "My soul has been rejected from peace; I have forgotten happiness. So I say, 'My strength has perished, and so my hope from the LORD'" (Lam. 3:17–18). In the poet's affliction, his memory weighed him down. "Surely my soul remembers and is bowed down within me" (Lam. 3:20). Memory sips on the cup of despondency. Despair drinks deeply. The "cudgel" of memory deals blow after blow.

But the poet does not remain in this dark place. Abruptly, he transitions, "This I recall to mind, therefore I have hope. The

9 Annie J. Flint, *He Giveth More Grace*, https://library.timelesstruths.org/music/He_Giveth_More_Grace/

LORD's lovingkindnesses indeed never cease, for His compassions never fail. They are new every morning; great is Your faithfulness" (Lam. 3:21–23). Miraculously, the same memory that weighed him down now lifted him up into hope-filled recollections of His loving, compassionate, and faithful God. A redeemed memory transformed a *millstone* of despair into a *milestone* of faith.

In 1865, Charles Spurgeon preached a sermon on this text. He commented, "That same recollection, which may, in its left hand, bring so many dark and gloomy omens, may be trained to bear in its right hand a wealth of hopeful signs. She need not wear a crown of iron; she may encircle her brow with a fillet of gold, all spangled with stars."[10] The same memory that served the cup of despondency now replaced it with a cup of hope. No new memory was formed. No new circumstances evolved to elicit this hope-filled response. Rather, Jeremiah "raked the ashes of the past"[11] to kindle a light of comfort for the present that would glow in the hope for the future. A redeemed memory ushered in hope as it shoved out the affliction of circumstance and pondered the changeless God. The thoughts of God filled the poet's mind and left no space for despair. He continues, "'The LORD is my portion,' says my soul, 'Therefore I have hope in Him'" (Lam. 3:24). A redeemed memory rightly rests in Him.

About a year after my family's fatal car accident, I started my medical school psychiatry rotation. For two months, I worked in a county hospital and saw many patients in crisis. On a late night, I remember sitting down across a table to interview a new patient for a suicide attempt. She not only shared a similar age to me but also experienced a recent death of her mom that left her devastated. Through her weeping, she whispered words of hopelessness. Life was no longer worth living. I listened and thought how easily this could have been me; and yet God's grace sustained and gave me hope, hope in Christ and the resurrection. Our two paths intersected that night in the hospital. We shared age and circumstance but differed in direction, one without hope and the other filled with hope.

Storm clouds sweep into life's journey in many shapes and

10 Charles H. Spurgeon, "Memory: The Handmaid of Hope," 15 October, 1865, Web. 1 May, 2021, spurgeon.org.

11 Ibid.

sizes. At the tip of South of Africa, a stretch of sea was so famous for its storms that the Portuguese sailors named it, "The Cape of Storms." However, after the cape was rounded, bolder navigators referred to it as "The Cape of Good Hope."[12] Similarly, a major storm in life can start out as "The Cape of Storms" but be redeemed into "The Cape of Good Hope." Redeemed memory recalls the storm with hope, not because the storm was any less severe. The storm did not change, but God also did not change. Hope springs from a memory of God in the midst of the storm who carried you through in His unceasing lovingkindness, unfailing compassion, and great faithfulness. The valley of trouble transforms into the door of hope (Hos. 2:15).

FAITH

Comfort draws from the past while hope dances in the future, but sanctifying faith ties the past and the future together. Faith looks to the past for courage and gazes to the future with conviction. As a young shepherd, David brought food to his brothers as they prepared to fight the Philistines. David heard Goliath taunt the living God. Unlike the Israelite army who trembled in fear, David shouted at the giant who taunted the living God. When brought to Saul, the king doubted David. David answered, "The LORD who delivered me from the paw of the lion and from the paw of the bear, He will deliver me from the hand of this Philistine" (1 Sam. 17:37).

Observe how David mined his memory from the past with the lion and bear for present courage with Saul and future faith against Goliath. David remembered the victorious outcomes of his battles with the lion and bear, and gave credit to the Lord for deliverance. How easy it is to give credit to self for those victories; or how easy is it to just forget these victories altogether in the face of a daunting trial? When trials come, memory so easily caters to doubt rather than to faith. "We generally inscribe our afflictions upon brass, while the records of the deliverances of God are written in water. It ought not to be! If our memories were more tenacious of the merciful visitations of our God, our

12 Charles H. Spurgeon, "Memory: The Handmaid of Hope," 15 October, 1865, Web. 1 May, 2021, *spurgeon.org*.

faith would often be strengthened in times of trial."[13] God uses redeemed memory through the Holy Spirit to kindle afresh these deliverances and strengthen faith. "Faith must make use of experiences and read them over unto God out of the register of a sanctified memory, as a recorder to Him who cannot forget."[14] In trials, the sun beats down and opens up cracks wider and wider in the mind for the rain of His grace to fall and soak deep down into your soul to water and grow faith.

Not to be missed, faith is not built only on the big events but rather nurtured in the ordinary circumstances of life. David's faith blossomed not only through the experience with the lion and the bear but through the mundane. Memory more easily recalls these extraordinary events, but memory must not miss the hand of God in the ordinary. It is in the ordinary that faith matures to be on full display in the extraordinary. "Let our faith be reared in the humble nursery of our daily little wants and trials; and then when need be it will come forth to do such great things that are required of it."[15] The little things combine and connect to form the scaffolding of faith for the big things. Sanctifying faith is a process with a timeline that joins the past with the future. Memories transformed into milestones of faith compel you to remember your redemption, your hope (Jer. 31:21).

ACTIONS

Redeemed memory produces the attitudes of humility, comfort, hope, and faith, and also results in actions. The actions of a redeemed memory revolve around a relationship with God and a relationship with others.

---

13 Charles H. Spurgeon, "The Lion-Slayer-The Giant Killer," 5 September, 1875, Web. 13 May, 2021, spurgeon.org.

14 Charles H. Spurgeon quotes Dickson in "Psalm 25," *The Treasury of David* vol. 1 (Thomas Nelson Publishers, 1984), 393.

15 Philip Bennett Power, *"I Will: Being the Determination of the Man of God as found in some of the "I Wills" of the Psalms.* (London: Wetheim, Macintosh, and Hunt, 1860), 63.

IMITATE GOD

A central action of a redeemed memory is imitation of God. You cannot imitate what you cannot remember. You cannot imitate Simon if you cannot remember what Simon says or does. Imitation implies importance. You only imitate what you deem worthy enough to be imitated, and God's greatness garners imitation. No greater example exists outside of Christ. "Therefore be imitators of God, as beloved children. And walk in love, as Christ loved us and gave Himself up for us, a fragrant offering and sacrifice to God" (Eph. 5:1–2). Imitation relies on remembrance; remember His love and imitate Christ's love to others.

Jesus provided examples to imitate from how to pray in the Lord's prayer (Matt. 6:9–13) and to how to serve with the washing of the disciples' feet (John 13:15). Jesus did not just tell His people to be holy but demonstrated how to be holy. The Son of Man, clothed in humanity, left an example "so that you might follow in His steps" (1 Peter 2:21). Jesus suffered well in the face of undeserved revilement and death. He not only provided an example at the cross to be imitated but also at the cross "bore our sins in His body on the tree, that we might die to sin and live to righteousness" (1 Peter 2:24). Christ made it possible through the cross for you to be able to imitate Him.

Some might view imitation as mechanical or robotic. Imitation of God is not a lifeless process but quite the opposite. Imitation of the Creator produces an explosion of creativity, not a stifling of it. To imitate utilizes imagination to "enter into the world of the one that is imitated. In imitation one takes up something of another person, but not in an inert, lifeless, mechanical sense; rather in the sense of its being...taken into ourselves and transformed."[16] The imitation of God transforms you from mediocrity into His likeness.

---

16 Ian McGilchrist, *The Master and His Emissary* (Yale University Press, 2019), 247–48.

CONFESS TO GOD

Confession is an action of redeemed memory. Confession of sin requires remembrance and acknowledgement of the sin itself. "If we say that we have no sin, we are deceiving ourselves and the truth is not in us" (1 John 1:8). It is a dangerous place to be when you no longer recognize and remember sin. Instead of confession, sin is concealed.

A woman came to the emergency department with concern for a breast complaint. When I walked into the room, I immediately smelled a foul odor, and her shirt was stained yellow. Six months ago, she noticed a mass in her right breast that worsened. Her flesh rotted to the point that part of the mass fell out. She placed it in a baggy in the freezer a month earlier but finally decided that day to get checked out as the smell was noticed by her family. The patient handed me the baggy with a grayish fulminating mass inside—end-stage cancer. Similarly, sin gets treated the same way—placed in a baggy in the freezer with the hope that everything will resolve. Instead of going to the Great Physician, the patient languishes at home.

The Holy Spirit, with use of the conscience, brings unrepentant sin to mind. God unsettles the sinner to seek help. David recalls, "When I kept silent about my sin, my body wasted away through my groaning all day long. For day and night Your hand was heavy upon me; my vitality was drained away as with the fever heat of summer" (Ps. 32:3–4). Better to be chastened than to be calloused. With David, the chastening produced confession. "I acknowledged my sin to You, and my iniquity I did not hide; I said, 'I will confess my transgressions to the LORD'; and You forgave the guilt of my sin (Ps. 32:5).'" Forgiveness removes the guilt and restores the soul. Sin is like a large sugary cake to a diabetic. It is consumed and puts the patient into a state of severe illness, even a coma. But confession is like insulin injected into the soul that revives you back to life.

David confessed his sin because he remembered the Good Physician and believed that "He is faithful and righteous to forgive us our sins and to cleanse us from all unrighteousness" (1 John 1:9). Confession is built upon relationship with God.

Sins of memory, like despair and doubt, thrive in a megaphone environment where you can only hear yourself and cannot hear any other source. These sins of memory drive confession away. You need to stop listening to yourself and start talking to God. Do not believe the lie that sin is unforgivable. Sin has limits, but His forgiveness is limitless.

PRAISE TO GOD

A forgiven soul is a thankful soul. Thanksgiving flows out of a redeemed memory. Remembrance of God's goodness leads to thankfulness for His provision. Christ exemplified this pattern of thanksgiving for meals, and Paul imitated this pattern even on a ship in the middle of a storm when he "took bread and gave thanks to God in the presence of all, and he broke it and began to eat" (Acts 27:35). Paul practiced prayer even in peril.

Spurgeon tells the story of "some good old woman in a cottage, who had nothing but a piece of bread and a little water, and lifting up her hands, she said, as a blessing, 'What! all this, and Christ too?'"[17] This woman manifested thankfulness from a contented spirit. She understood that "contentment is not by addition but by subtraction: seeking to add a thing will not bring contentment. Instead, subtracting from your desires until you are satisfied only with Christ brings contentment."[18] The soul is satisfied in Christ alone.

A practice of praise in daily habits permeates throughout life in the good times and bad times. The circumstances that surround the believer shift and change, but the Lord remains good and unchanged. True thanksgiving expresses not just what you are thankful for but whom you are thankful to. God is the focal point and recipient of praise. The Christian cries out, "Oh give thanks to the LORD, call upon His name; make known His deeds among the peoples. Sing to Him, sing praises to Him; speak of all His wonders" (Ps. 105:1–2). Connect the gift to the Giver.

Praise serves as an anecdote for many of the miseries of

17 Charles H. Spurgeon, "The Peculiar Sleep of the Beloved," 4 March, 1885, Web. 22 July, 2021, spurgeon.org.

18 Jeremiah Burroughs, *The Rare Jewel of Christian Contentment* (CreatedSpace Independent Publishing, 2013), 19.

memory like despair, regret, and grumbling. When stuck in the slime of despondency, praise requires persistence and discipline to recall to mind. Once the first words of praise are uttered, the rest start to quickly follow—and the dam is unleashed. Memory then overflows with eager utterances of His goodness like the psalmist: "They shall eagerly utter the memory of Your abundant goodness and will shout joyfully of Your righteousness" (Ps. 145:7). Instead of sitting in the slime of despondency, you now splash in the pool of praise.

Praise and pleasure go hand in hand. C.S. Lewis insightfully wrote, "I think we delight to praise what we enjoy because the praise not merely expresses but completes the enjoyment; it is its appointed consummation."[19] Enjoyment elicits praise; and praise completes the enjoyment. Memory plays a vital role then in both praise and enjoyment. "A pleasure is full grown only when it is remembered."[20] Pleasure and memory are not distinct entities but intertwined. C.S. Lewis continues,

> When you and I met, the meeting was over very shortly, it was nothing. Now it is growing something as we remember it. But still we know very little about it. What it will be when I remember it as I lie down to die, what it makes in me all my days till then—that is the real meeting. The other is only the beginning of it.[21]

Memory harmonizes praise and pleasure through the passage of time. Praise and pleasure interplay with each other in a symphony of joyful sound.

Songbirds create rich and diverse music by the use of not just one membrane but two. The second membrane, called the syrinx, vibrates with airflow at incredibly fast speeds up to one hundred times faster than the human eye blinks. Select songbirds can vibrate these two membranes independently to produce two different notes at the same time, one at a low frequency and the second at a high frequency to create up to thirty-six notes per

19 C. S. Lewis, *Reflection on the Psalms* (Inspirational Press, 1994), 179.
20 C. S. Lewis, *Out of the Silent Planet* (Pan Books Limited, 1960), 48.
21 Ibid.

second.[22] So it is with pleasure and praise. Each fires in harmony with the other to produce joy. A redeemed memory is a joy-filled memory.

LOVE OTHERS

A redeemed memory induces action not just toward God but also toward others. The right remembrance of God leads to a right remembrance of others. Many commands that direct actions toward others spring from God's actions toward you.

The disciple whom Jesus loved, John, leans on this pattern of an indicative driving an imperative when he writes, "In this is love, not that we loved God, but that He loved us and sent His Son to be the propitiation for our sins. Beloved, if God so loved us, we also ought to love one another" (1 John 4:10–11). Love for others comes from a remembrance of His love for us. The command to love others comes from a remembrance of God's love for you.

When remembered rightly, the love of Christ removes indifference toward others and replaces it with involvement even to the point of self-sacrifice. B.B. Warfield connects this self-sacrifice to "forgetfulness of self in others. It means entering into every man's hopes and fears, longings and despairs.... It means not that we should live one life but a thousand lives, binding ourselves to a thousand souls by the filaments of so loving a sympathy that their lives become ours."[23] Warfield highlights the work of a redeemed memory in loving others in self-forgetfulness. Forgetfulness of self, coupled to a remembrance of Christ, shapes memory so that you love in a sacrificial way that defies worldly sense. "We know love by this, that He laid down His life for us; and we ought to lay down our lives for the brethren" (1 John 3:16). In a world of self-promotion and self-preservation, redeemed memory stands out for its irrationality. But the Christian is simply following Christ's example of extreme self-sacrifice as He died not for the righteous or even a good man but for vile sinners (see Rom. 5:7–8) that includes you and me.

Love, then, does not only get directed toward friends but

---

22 Jennifer Ackerman, *The Genius of Birds* (Penguin Books, 2017), 143.

23 B. B. Warfield, *The Person and Work of Christ* (P&R Publishing, 1950), 574.

toward all including the downcast and rejected, the prisoners (Heb. 13:3) and the poor (Gal. 2:10). My dad used to say, "Love the unlovely." Cleaner fish are a group of fish that remove the dead skin and parasites from others. These fish can clean up to two thousand other fish a day. Cleaner fish actually prefer the dirtiest fish, the ones with the highest parasitic load.[24] In a study where the cleaner fish were removed from the reef, the parasite load for the average fish increased 4.5 fold in only twelve hours.[25] The cleaner fish provide a great example of how to love the unlovely. Be attracted to those who bear the crushing parasitic burdens. But beware of the saber-toothed blennies who mimic the cleaner fish. Dirty fish come to the blennies to be cleaned. The blennies lure the unsuspecting close until they take a bite off of a fin and swim for cover.[26] The selfish hypocrite will offer to help but instead hurt others, including the unlovely. Be a cleaner fish, not a blennie.

The gospel helps to redeem memory to remember others for their best moments and not their worst; however, it may be that some people are simply enemies without any best moments. Are enemies excluded from the commands to love? Ultimately, love for others extends beyond the unlovely to the unloving (enemies). As mentioned, Christ died for you when you were His enemy, and He then commands you to "love your enemies and pray for those who persecute you" (Matt. 5:44). This is only possible with a transformed heart and mind guided by the Holy Spirit. These actions are not easy, but God did not call you to a life of ease but a life of sacrifice.

SHARE WITH OTHERS

An action that results from a redeemed memory is sharing the good news of the gospel with others. Loving others compels you to share with them what you value the most. The one who loves others does not withhold Christ's love on the cross but invites others to share in its joys.

24 A. S. Grutter, "Relationship between cleaning rates and ectoparasite loads in coral reef fishes," *Marine Ecology Progress Series*, vol. 118 (1995), 51–58.

25 A. S. Grutter, "Cleaner fish really do clean," *Nature*, vol. 398 (1999), 672–73.

26 Jonathan Balcombe, *What a Fish Knows*, Scientific American, 2017, 158.

In the time of Elisha, the Arameans laid siege to the city of Samaria. Conditions grew so severe that people ate donkey dung and boiled their own babies (2 Kings 6:24–30). By His own power, God disrupted the Arabian camp and the army fled, leaving their food and spoils behind. Out of desperation, four lepers left Samaria and walked to the enemy camp, only to find it abandoned. They feasted and carried away the abandoned treasure of silver and gold. "Then they said to one another, 'We are not doing right. This is a day of good news, but we are keeping silent'" (2 Kings 7:9a). The lepers went and told the gatekeepers of the city the good news of freedom and riches. These lepers remembered their former, hopeless condition in the city and could not keep the newfound wealth to themselves. A redeemed memory does not keep selfishly silent but proclaims the riches of the gospel. "Get yourself up on a high mountain, O Zion, bearer of good news" (Isa. 40:9a) and lift up your voice and proclaim that the victory has been won. Enter through the narrow gate and discover the riches procured for you in Christ. Leave the donkey dung, and feast on the delights of Christ.

These lepers would likely share this story of deliverance time and time again; and so, too, the good news of the gospel must be repeated in the same way. Paul reminded the Corinthians of the gospel they had received "that Christ died for our sins according to the Scriptures, and that He was buried, and that He was raised on the third day according to the Scriptures" (1 Cor. 15:3–4). This outline of the gospel message requires repeating, even if it is familiar.

A redeemed memory not only declares the gospel to others but defends the gospel against others. When the gospel is shared, some will believe, but many will reject it. Memory brings readiness "to make a defense to everyone who asks you to give an account for the hope that is in you" (1 Peter 3:15). In gentleness, boldly testify to the truth. The declaration and defense of the gospel both hinge on the same powerful message of God's grace.

COMFORT OTHERS

Redeemed memory plays a role in the final action toward others to be discussed—the comfort of others. Paul insightfully writes, "Blessed be the God and Father of our Lord Jesus Christ, the Father of mercies and God of all comfort, who comforts us in all our affliction so that we will be able to comfort those who are in any affliction with the comfort with which we ourselves are comforted by God" (1 Cor. 1:3–4). The pattern looks familiar here as the command to comfort others grows out of the comfort God provides you. In the midst of wandering through your own wilderness of affliction, the last thing to enter the mind is how this affliction will give future opportunities to serve and comfort others. And yet, when time passes and healing follows, comforting others is one of the sweetest benefits of past suffering.

Suffering produces compassion, moving a person from simply pitying another to prompting to act in mercy to meet a need. This is especially true in grief. Memory recalls not just the pain and deep emptiness in death but also God's grace and comfort in time of need. A redeemed memory moves with compassion toward the one who is now grief-stricken, both in understanding the pain and also in knowing the hope. God equips the one who suffered in the past to now provide comfort to another in the present. Only God can transform a past sufferer into a present comforter.

Chapter 8
Application Questions

1. How does humility connect with other fruits of memory like comfort, hope, and faith?

2. What role does memory play in grief? How does God provide comfort in the midst of pain?

3. Do you find yourself slow to confess sin? How does redeemed memory help with confession?

4. Do you consider yourself a thankful person? Consider writing down your complaints and then writing down your praises. Make observations on the length of the list and what is included. Are there any surprises?

5. How can you serve others with a redeemed memory?

6. What is the link between being comforted and comforting? Have you ever suffered and then had an opportunity to comfort another person who was suffering?

9

Man's Corruption of Future Remembrance

Most people relegate memory to things of the past. However, memory plays a vital role in the future and how it shapes present living for future remembrance. Future remembrance refers to how a person is remembered after death.

As discussed previously, the fall of man brought sin and death into the world. Memory was not spared from the effects of the curse. Memory distorts a person's thinking, bending it toward self and away from God. In future remembrance, the same inward curve manifests with a bend into self, a desire to extend your time beyond the days allotted on earth into the future. This idolatrous tendency seeks to leave something behind, a type of immortality. The Cambridge Dictionary defines immortality as "the quality of being very special and famous and therefore likely to be remembered for a long time."[1] This thirst for immortality through memory attempts to prolong remembrance into the future after death.

---

1 "Immortality," dictionary.cambridge.org, accessed 14 June, 2021.

EVIDENCE OF DISTORTED FUTURE REMEMBRANCE IN CULTURE

Who's Who books demonstrate the world's obsession with future remembrance. The goal of these books is to compile lists of individuals who are noteworthy and influential. These books attempt to memorialize the influential living for present and future readers. The first who's who book, 250 pages long, appeared in 1849 in the UK.[2] These lists exploded in popularity with over 286 lists.[3] The interest in these books is not to read them but to be included in them.

The desire to be recognized as significant expands into awards. Hollywood etches a name on a star on the fifteen-block "Walk of Fame." This practice originated to "maintain the glory of a community whose name means glamour and excitement in the four corners of the world."[4] The stars etched in the pavement remind the pedestrian of the significance of the one they tread on. Hollywood compliments this practice with honors like the lifetime achievement award given posthumously. These awards preserve the accomplishments of the actor or actress for years to come. By recognizing lifetime contributions of the dead, the living legitimize the significance of their own current work.

Similarly, sport seeks to enshrine players. Every major sport has built a Hall of Fame that includes the most notable players with memorabilia and plaques that recount their accomplishments. The present players look back to the past players who were honored and hope one day to create their own legacy. The Hall of Fame perpetuates the praise from the playing days to after the player passes away. It extends the cheers from the stands by fans who witnessed the great play to future fans who never watched the player at all. Yet, no matter how hard the world tries, the applause fades away.

---

2 Ernie Smith, "The Weird, Vain History of Who's Who Books," accessed 14 June, 2021, atlasobscura.com.

3 Ibid.

4 "History of the Walk of Fame," accessed 14 June, 2021, walkoffame.com.

EVIDENCE OF DISTORTED FUTURE REMEMBRANCE IN SELF

If you are not on the *Who's Who* list, a Hollywood movie star, or a professional sports athlete, do not be tempted to dismiss the evidence of distorted future remembrance. This obsession with the preservation of memory on earth beyond the grave exists inside of each of us. Each image-bearer longs for his image to remain forever on the earth.

Photography

Photography is one way for image perpetuity. Cameras preserve moments through pictures. Pictures are irreplaceable, since the moment can never be recreated. In a desire to preserve special moments, photographers invade those moments with interruptions to try to get the perfect shot, to the point that the picture might be prized above the actual moment itself. Too many times, the moment is experienced through the camera lens or phone screen. Scientific studies show that media diminishes the precision of memory by distracting you from the details of the sounds and sights.[5] Ironically, in trying to preserve memories with media, memory for the moment declines.

Beyond the constant taking of photos, a high value is placed on the preservation and storage of photos. In my childhood home, the photo albums were stored in the living room on the bottom shelf of a bookcase. The living room was located in the center of the house and served as a central meeting place. Here, the photo albums collected dust until someone would pull one out and reminisce. Each of the kids would want to see his or her baby photos, and each would hear his or her birth story. The photos prompted storytelling and community.

In the case of a disaster like a fire, many would grab photo albums in fear of losing these special story-prompting photos. When Hurricane Rita approached Houston in 2005, my wife and I packed up the car with our most precious possessions, and the entire middle seat of the small sedan was packed with

5 Diana L. Tami, et al, "Media Usage Diminishes Memory for Experiences" Journal of Experimental Social Psychology, vol. 76 (May 2018), 161–68.

my family's photo albums. In this last decade, digital photos have altered photographic storage. Backup hard drives and storage in multiple digital spaces highlight the continued value placed on photos. This is not to say that photos do not have a place to rekindle joyous moments, but they need not be elevated to such an importance that the shiny images are now idols, symbols of a deeper fight for permanence and preservation.

Childbearing

Besides photography, the preservation of name lurks in the shadows of childbearing. What better way to prolong time on the earth than through descendants that extend the family name? In selfishness, you pervert the command to multiply and fill the earth with God's image to your own image. Absalom, the son of King David, shared this corruption of future remembrance. He had "set up for himself a pillar which is in the King's Valley, for he said, 'I have no son to preserve my name.' So he named the pillar after his own name, and it is called Absalom's Monument to this day" (2 Sam. 18:18). He feared future forgetfulness without an heir and built a monument dedicated to himself to likely serve as a burial plot. Absalom showed more care about his dead body than his living soul. He lived a rebellious life that led to his demise. Instead of his body being buried at his monument, his body was taken by Joab's men where they "cast him into a deep pit in the forest and erected over him a very great heap of stones" (2 Sam. 18:17a). Matthew Henry notes, "Travelers say that the place is taken notice of to this day, and that it is common for passengers to throw a stone to this heap with words to this purport: Cursed be the memory of Absalom...."[6] Absalom accomplished his desire for his name to be preserved; but instead of honor, his name is buried under a heap of disgrace.

6 Matthew Henry, "2 Samuel 18," in *Matthew Henry's Commentary,* vol. 2 (MacDonald Publishing Company, 1980), 540.

Honor
•••••••••

The final evidence for the distortion of future remembrance closely ties in with Absalom's story as there is a desire not just to be remembered but to be honored in future remembrance. The desire to live honorably and be honored in death is not inherently wrong unless the honor is sought to gain men's favor and not God's. When the purpose to living is to be honored by men in dying, failure ensues.

If meaning is measured by the number of people who attend a memorial service, then the measurement is incorrect. This measurement does not reflect the impact of an older, faithful saint who moves late in life to be cared for by family, and who outlives friends and dies in relative obscurity in a nursing home. D. A. Carson recounts the death of his father, Tom, in these words: "When he died, there were no crowds outside the hospital, no editorial comments in the papers, no announcements on television, no mention in Parliament, no attention paid by the nation. In his hospital room there was no one by his bedside."[7] Tom Carson was an ordinary pastor who died in obscurity. Does this mean his life was insignificant? No.

For memory of you to exist beyond your lifespan requires someone else who outlives you to remember and retell your story. Death demands a narrator to carry on your story.

DEATH AND DISTORTED FUTURE REMEMBRANCE

Future remembrance by others only exists because of death. Death, the end of the earthly race of self, requires someone else to remember you after you are gone, to pick up the baton of memory and carry it beyond your finish line at the grave. Future remembrance relies on others. The self-sufficient now transitions to the self-dependent.

To better understand the present corruption of future remembrance, the first step is to examine death, the catalyst for future remembrance. Death casts a shadow of fear over life. The

7 D. A. Carson, *Memoirs of an Ordinary Pastor* (Wheaton, IL: Crossway, 2008), 147–48.

writer of Hebrews refers to the fear of death as lifelong slavery (Heb. 2:15). The fear of death sits at the core of a corrupted view of future remembrance.

Death is unmistakable
••••••••••••••••••••••••••••••

Death does not need an introduction. Everyone knows death when he sees it or even smells it. In the emergency room, a ring-down from EMS interrupts the drones of a typical day. A fifty-three-year-old was found down without a pulse. CPR is in progress, and sirens announce the arrival. Despite best efforts with CPR, lines, and tubes, the bedside ultrasound shows a still heart. The time of death is pronounced fifteen minutes later by me, but everyone knows. It is astonishing how quickly the room transitions from a flurry to a stillness and how quickly the body goes from life to non-life. The color changes; the sparkle extinguishes. The body is now an unoccupied shell.

Death is universal
••••••••••••••••••••••••••

Dust to dust (Eccl. 3:20). While living, the return to dust is already taking place. An adult produces about one pound of dust per year with at least half the dust in the home deposited from skin cells.[8] Every time the vacuum bag is emptied, the dust reminds of future, inevitable demise. The Bible affirms, "It is appointed for men to die once" (Heb. 9:27a). Each human is ordained one life and one death (except Enoch and Elijah). You only enter the world one way, but you can exit the world a variety of ways, with over eight thousand possible coded diagnoses at death.[9] You elude all but one in the end.

Death is irreversible
••••••••••••••••••••••••••••••

Death does not have a do over button. It is irreversible. Resurrections in the Bible might argue against finality; but in the end,

8 J. Van Bronswijk, *House Dust Biology for Allergists, Acarologists and Mycologists* (NIB Publishers, 1981), 37.

9 Kathryn Schulz, "Final Forms: What death certificates tells us, and what they can't," *The New Yorker* (April 7, 2014), 38–39.

Lazarus died. Lazarus is not walking the streets of Judea today. Medicine gives the illusion of the possibility of being saved. The pulseless regain a pulse. The comatose recover cognition. The blue breathe again. But even those who recover eventually succumb. Escape once or twice, but not forever.

Death is uncontrollable
••••••••••••••••••••••••••••

Despite best efforts like diet, exercise, and healthy living, death is uncontrollable. In the ER, I have taken care of the marathon runner on a Mediterranean diet who died from a heart attack in his forties. This example does not diminish the need to care for the body but illustrates the timing of death is not up to you. Just as you did not choose the day of your birth, so you do not choose your day of death (Eccl. 8:8).

Death is unexpected
••••••••••••••••••••••••••••

Death is certain, but the timing is not. Each day could be the last. "In the midst of life we are in death, just one step away from eternity."[10] Approximately ten percent of deaths are sudden and unexpected.[11] These deaths include things like heart attacks or car accidents like the one that involved my family. Death is a shock but not just for ten percent. Even for those who carry a diagnosis like cancer with prolonged decline, the actual day of death is still surprising because it is unnatural, not a part of the original design of creation. The un-design of creation instills fear, that something is not right.

Time is not evil. It was created good by the timeless God to be enjoyed. But with sin, time no longer ticks forward in joyful expectation but rushes toward fearful separation. "As for the days of our life, they contain seventy years, or if due to strength, eighty years, yet their pride is but labor and sorrow; for soon it is gone, and we fly away" (Ps. 90:10). Awareness of the brevity of time is heightened by the understanding that God

10 J. I. Packer, *Fundamentalism and the Word of God* (Inter-Varsity Press, 1958), 14.

11 Mary Elizabeth Lewis, et al, "Estimated incidence and risk factors of sudden unexpected death," *Open heart,* vol. 3,1 e000321, 23 March, 2016.

"has also set eternity" in the heart of man. Man senses eternity but faces a short lifespan. "The time is short, and upon this small wire of time hangs the weight of eternity."[12] Life is short, but it matters.

Death is unsettling
••••••••••••••••••••••••

Death rattles and displaces normalcy. A husband who loses a wife does not simply reset to an earlier phase in life when he was single. He no longer enjoys the deep relationship with the one he loved who is irreplaceable. Death leaves the one behind longing for one more glance, one more laugh, one more story, one more ordinary day. It unsettles the ordinary.

Summary

Death is unmistakable, universal, irreversible, uncontrollable, unexpected, and unsettling. For these reasons, and many more, death elicits fear. This fear of death runs deep as it strikes at the core of a human being—the desire for self-preservation and the acknowledgement that, one day, self will no longer be an active presence. Death is the transition point from making memories to being a memory.

UNDERLYING FEARS OF DISTORTED FUTURE REMEMBRANCE

Death brings about future remembrance, which rests upon the memories of others to tell your story. In the finale song of *Hamilton*, the cast sings these lines that hit upon this theme:

And when you're gone
Who remembers your name
Who keeps your flame
Who tells your story?[13]

12 Thomas Watson, "Time's Shortness," accessed 21 April, 2021, gracegems.org.
13 Lin-Manuel Miranda, "Who Lives, Who Dies, Who Tells Your Story," *Hamilton*, 2015.

These lines capture the tension of future remembrance; the burden to tell your story rests on the memory of others. This future reliance on others leads to fears of fiction, dishonor, futility, and insignificance.

Fear of fiction

What if others do remember me in the future but in a fictitious way? When a loved one dies, the memories especially of last moments solidify; but over time, even these powerful memories dwindle. The ones left behind must continue to reconstruct the life lived, and imperfect memory is susceptible to fiction. After the death of his wife, C.S. Lewis observed,

> Already, less than a month after her death, I can feel the slow, insidious beginning of a process that will make the H. I think of into a more and more imaginary woman. Founded on fact, no doubt. I shall put in nothing fictitious (or I hope I shan't). But won't the composition inevitably become more and more my own? The reality is no longer there to check me, to pull me up short, as the real H. so often did, so unexpectedly, by being so thoroughly herself and not me. [14]

Without the real person present, the living loved one selects the pieces that form the image of the one who is gone. Even with good intentions and diligent effort, the image is imperfect with misshapen pieces and pieces missing altogether.

The fiction in remembrance strikes fear not just for the loved one but also for the one who is inaccurately portrayed in a negative light. A story attaches to a person that is intentionally or unintentionally fabricated that tarnishes future remembrance. The dead man who is defamed is unable to defend himself against any indictments. He relies on others to the denounce the slander of his character.

---

14 C. S. Lewis, *A Grief Observed.* (Faber and Faber, 1964), 8.

Fear of dishonor

What if others accurately remember the dishonorable things I really did do? The Bible gives example after example of those who are remembered infamously for significant sins that defined their unrepentant lives. King Jehoram "departed with no one's regret, and they buried him in the city of David, not in the tombs of the kings" (2 Chron. 21:20). The dishonor of Jehoram remains to this day through the biblical recounting of his life. The most famous traitor in the Bible is Judas. The dishonor associated with the betrayer of Jesus is so well known that his name, Judas, is synonymous with a traitor even today. In the case of dishonor, forgetfulness might be the preference.

Fear of futility

In contrast, what if others forget the honorable things I did? Solomon touches on this aspect when he writes, "There was a small city with few men in it and a great king came to it, surrounded it, and constructed large siege works against it. But there was found in it a poor wise man and he delivered the city by his wisdom. Yet no one remembered that poor man" (Eccl. 2:14–15). The heroic and honorable feats of men fade away. Like the troubadour of the Middle Ages, the songs of chivalry are no longer sung, lost in the ripples of time. Even the contributions of Herman Ebbinghaus are relatively unknown. Who is Dr. Ebbinghaus? He is the forgotten "father of memory," who pioneered the early scientific studies on human memory in the nineteenth century.[15]

Similarly, the disappearance of the remembrance of honorable things also includes the dishonorable things as well. Judas is famous, but many fools will die and their foolishness dies away with them. Solomon considers the matter: "For there is no lasting remembrance of the wise man as with the fool, inasmuch as in the coming days all will be forgotten. And how the wise man and the fool alike die" (Eccl. 2:16). Futility asks, "Does it really matter what you did, honorable or dishonorable, if no remembers it?" Death erases deeds.

15 "Ebbinghaus, Herman," accessed 25 June, 2021, encyclopedia.com.

Fear of insignificance
•••••••••••••••••••••••••••

What if others do not just forget the deeds I did but also forget me? Here is the pinnacle of the fear of future remembrance—insignificance. Remembrance represents some form of permanence. David writes, "As for man, his days are like grass; as a flower of the field so he flourishes. When the wind has passed over it, it is no more, and its place acknowledges it no longer" (Ps. 103:15–16). Time and place both forsake man in death. He is no more. Grass manifests this cycle of impermanence—the sprouting, the scorching, and the ceasing to be. "Man lives on the grass and lives like the grass.... If he lives out his little day, he is cut down at last, and it is far more likely that he will wither before he comes to maturity, or be plucked away on a sudden, long before he has fulfilled his time."[16] As the grass dies, nature continues on its course without missing a beat as the sun rises, the rain falls, and the wind blows. Even the forget-me-not flower fades away.

Each life leaves impressions like footprints on a sandy beach. Dig your heels in deep, but, in the end, two or three waves later the footprint is gone without a trace. Similarly, in two or three generations, no one will remember you. In fact, memory by others will fade faster than the body decomposes. Decomposition of bones to dust in a sealed coffin can take decades[17] while the average grave is visited for only about fifteen years.[18] Solomon warns, "There is no remembrance of earlier things; and also of the later things which will occur, there will be for them no remembrance among those who will come later still" (Eccl. 1:11). Who is going to tell your story? Nobody. Your dust will disappear without a trace (Ps. 104:29; Eccl. 12:7).

EFFECTS OF DISTORTED FUTURE REMEMBRANCE

The underlying fears of death, dishonor, futility, and insignificance poison future remembrance. The distortion of future re-

16 Charles H. Spurgeon, "Psalm 103," in *The Treasury of David*, vol. 2 (Thomas Nelson Publishers, 1984), 281.

17 Arpad A. Vass, "Dust to Dust," *Scientific American*, vol. 303, No. 3, 58.

18 Harry Mount, "Espirit de Corpse," *Literary Review*, May 2013.

membrance is not isolated to the theoretical tomorrow but invades every crevice of daily living. The same gravitational force of self that bends present memory toward the self also influences future remembrance as it seeks to perpetuate the future self after death. As the prospects of future remembrance are threatened, fears emerge. In response to these fears, the effects of a distorted remembrance may be classified into the hyperactivity of heroism, hedonism, and hoarding, or the inactivity of anxiety and apathy.

HYPERACTIVE EFFECTS OF DISTORTED FUTURE REMEMBRANCE

Fear stimulates the release of adrenaline, the body's means to summon extra strength to escape ruin. In the case of the fears of future remembrance, a person fights for purpose and the preservation of self. Life revolves around self. Like the sun, the gravitational forces of self seek to pull everything else around into orbit with itself as the center. The universe cannot continue without you at the center; all will collapse. A person will do everything he can in the present to combat the future threat to self.

Heroism

The first way to preserve self into the future is heroism. Heroism carries the idea of doing great things in order to be remembered by others on earth. A Christian desires to make a meaningful spiritual contribution to be praised by men. Perhaps his or her name and heroic deeds for God will be passed on to future generations through a written biography. The aspiration to be biographical is mingled with potentially good means to do great spiritual things. However, the person is motivated to bring future glory to self and not to God.

The Bible, a compilation of historical biographies, provides example after example of leaders who were prepared to lead God's people through humbling paths. These leaders, like shepherds Moses and David, did not choose their courses; rather God refined them through hardship that produced humility. These leaders did not perform heroic acts for themselves; they performed them for God.

In contrast, Luke wrote about Simon the magician who was "astonishing the people of Samaria, claiming to be someone great; and they all, from smallest to greatest, were giving attention to him, saying, 'This man is what is called the Great Power of God'" (Acts 8:9b–10). After the good news was preached by Philip, many believed. Philip performed miracles, which validated the message, and the Holy Spirit was received. Simon desired this God-given power and offered money for it. Peter strongly rebuked him. Simon desired a good thing but for wrong motives. He desired heroic power but for personal greatness.

Pride is the carbon dioxide of sin. It is not outside of you to be breathed in like oxygen but rather produced within you and exhaled outward. If pride is retained inside of you to such a high level, it can kill you.

Heroism demonstrates the strong desire inside of you to earn favor by yourself and for yourself, to attain significance by your own deeds and bypass God's grace. The hero thinks his legacy will not only be left on earth but hopes his greatness will even rise to heaven. The hero tries to climb Jacob's ladder all the way to the throne room of God to earn a seat of honor in heaven. By seeking meaning in only the heroic acts, a Christian overlooks the ways to serve that catch God's eye in the form of small things like a cup of cold water or a widow's mite. The Son of Man did not come to earth "to be served but to serve" (Matt. 20:28). The Son of Man, a true hero and Savior of the world, conquered self.

Hedonism

The fears from a distorted future remembrance also underlie hedonism, the pursuit of pleasure. The inevitable end of self leads to a focus on self-happiness in the present. The mind occupies itself with many matters that just don't matter. The parade of entertainment distracts from the sobriety of death. Solomon recorded his experimentation with pleasure as he did not refuse himself anything that he desired. He tested pleasure, and it was futile (Eccl. 2:1). He concluded pleasure did not accomplish anything (Eccl. 2:1).

Hedonism results from the inward workings of a familiar

foe—fulfillment of self in self. These pleasures appeal to the deep-seated inward longing to be happy and satisfied. Such pleasures destroy you much like the way the jeweled caterpillar is destroyed. Known for its beautiful appearance, a pearly substance with spikes covers its half-inch-long body. These spikes easily break off and deter predators, like ants, by gumming up their mouths with the sticky substance like an old caramel candy. Despite this protection, the caterpillar has a weakness: the under-belly is unprotected. A maggot of the Tachinid fly sneaks under and drills into the jeweled caterpillar.[19] As the caterpillar feeds, the maggot grows and then consumes the caterpillar from the inside out. In a similar way, the pleasures of this world find the under belly of the believer: they sneak into the soft part of the heart and take up residence. What starts as a simple joy soon displaces the Ultimate Joy: Jesus Christ.

Hoarding
. . . .

The hyperactivity of hoarding to amass earthly treasure results from a shortsightedness for the future. Creation's hoarder, the bowerbird, collects shiny treasures to adorn his nest. The bird prefers to nest close to garbage dumps with easy access to metal objects like small matchbox cars to put on display. The treasures are arranged by larger birds with the smallest treasures placed closest to the entrance to make the bird appear more impressive.[20] The nests are oriented from north to south in order to illuminate the display in full sunlight to attract females. How often do you spend time in the garbage dump picking out shiny objects for vain purposes?

Vain riches may quickly vanish even through spending, bad investing, or stealing (Eccl. 5:14). Thomas Watson observed, "Worldly things are like a fair picture drawn on the ice—which the sun quickly melts."[21] If riches are not lost during life, then riches vanish at death. Death untethers treasure.

In hoarding, you convince yourself of permanent

19 Matt Simon, "Absurd Creature of the Week: It's Not a Jewel—It's the World's Most Stunning Caterpillar," accessed 5 July, 2021, wired.com 30 Oct 2015.

20 Jennifer Ackerman, *The Genius of Birds* (Penguin Books, 2017), 180.

21 Thomas Watson, "Time's Shortness," accessed 5 July, 2021, gracegems.org.

ownership. You might acknowledge that God owns the cattle on a thousand hills (Ps. 50:10) while still secretly believing you own the cattle on hill one thousand and one. Death reminds each person he is a temporary borrower even of the cattle on hill one thousand and one. At death, the hoarded treasure passes into another borrower's hands who did not work for it. "Thus I hated all the fruit of my labor for which I had labored under the sun, for I must leave it to the man who will come after me" (Eccl. 2:18). The hoarder who spent his whole life accumulating now gives it to another. Death peels back the fingers of the miser.

Just as riches fade away, so do the rich themselves. "For the sun rises with a scorching wind and withers the grass; and its flower falls off and the beauty of its appearance is destroyed; so too the rich man in the midst of his pursuits will fade away" (James 1:11). The hoarder and the giver share the same fate.

INACTIVE EFFECTS OF DISTORTED FUTURE REMEMBRANCE

Fear not only stirs up a response of hyperactivity but also of inactivity. Inactivity arrives in the form of anxiety and apathy. In anxiety, the mind runs but the body remains paralyzed; in apathy, the mind and body remain aloof, defensively disengaged.

Anxiety

Just as death awaits every living being in the future, so anxiety is future oriented. Instead of thinking on "What is," the mind dwells on "What if?" You worry that tomorrow will not look as bright as today; or even more concerning, tomorrow will not exist. Anxiety about tomorrow robs you of the joy today. Will tomorrow be there to be enjoyed? Charles Taylor writes that there is a fear and anxiety that "our actions, goals, achievements, and life, have a lack of weight, gravity, thickness, substance. There is a deeper resonance which they lack, which we feel should be there."[22] The fear of insignificance leads to anxiety.

22 Charles Taylor, *A Secular Age* (Belknap Press, 2018), 307.

Anxiety spins the mind round and round and burdens the worrier with the hypothetical. The mind races. The heart races. The lungs race. The rest of the body remains motionless, imprisoned without a way of escape. Constant reminders point to the inevitable end. "Normal" aging with a wearing out of joints, eyes, ears, and memories points to mortality. "If we look at ourselves, we bear Death's signs and tokens about us in every part of our body."[23] Death in the ear (deafness) and death in the eye (blindness) signal death of the body is near. Anxiety erupts from these signs and symptoms of inevitable death.

In the emergency room, it is quite common to evaluate a patient for a panic attack but also for anxiety about symptoms that might indicate an underlying bad disease. A man in his sixties would arrive at any time of the day or night for a daily assessment for left shoulder pain. He was convinced that this was a sign of a heart attack. He would tell me he would rather be safe than sorry as he did not want to die. Even if he came to the emergency room every day, eventually this man would die. Anxiety rarely provides a benefit, but it always provides a burden. Like Augustine quips, "Among the daily chances of life every man on earth is threatened in the same way by innumerable deaths, and it is uncertain which of them will come to him. And so the question is whether it is better to suffer one in dying or to fear them all in living."[24]

Apathy

....

Anxiety and apathy are not exclusive to each other. In fact, Pascal connects the two in this observation in *Pensees*:

> They fear the most trifling things, foresee and feel them; and the same man who spends so many days and nights in fury and despair at losing some office or at some imaginary affront to his honor is the very one who knows that he is going to lose everything through death but feels neither anxiety nor emotion. It is a monstrous thing to see one and the same

23 Charles H. Spurgeon, "Memento Mori." 18 March, 1860, Web. 5 July 2021, spurgeon.org

24 Augustine, *City of God* (Christian Classics Ethereal Library, 1890), 24.

heart at once so sensitive to minor things and so strangely insensitive to the greatest.[25]

Here is a mystery—that you can be anxious about small things but apathetic toward the greatest thing: death. The lack of concern and contemplation of death is a common complacency of the mind. Death is for others and not for me; or as Tolstoy wrote in *The Death of Ivan Ilyich*, death "evoked in them all the usual feeling of relief that it was someone else, not they, who had died."[26] You recognize others' mortality and reassure yourself of your own immortality. Apathy is an effort to maintain peace by thoughtlessness, but, "If I do not think of death, yet death will think of me."[27]

At funerals and times of mourning when the mind should be engaged, thoughts of death quickly slip away. The funeral of another should serve as "a looking-glass in which you may see your own dying face."[28] The fleeting thought reflects the fleeting life. John Calvin writes, "We form all our plans just as if we had fixed our immortality on the earth. If we see a funeral, or walk among graves, as the image of death is then present to the eye… our philosophy is momentary and the thought of perpetuity still keeps hold of our minds."[29] Funerals and graves may help briefly orient (Eccl. 7:2), but today the funeral has been replaced by a celebration; and the church graveyards have been replaced by parking lots and playgrounds. Despite the presence of death in funerals, many people refuse to contemplate the subject until lying on a deathbed like Ivan Ilyich, waiting till the weakest and most chaotic moment in life to look death in the face.

Modern medicine encourages apathy. Death is now handled by the doctors in the hospital, removed from the family in the home. The veil of the hospital curtain is pulled to guard the eyes of the curious and detach the hearts of the caring. Hiding death

25 Blaise Pascal, *Pensees,* trans. A. J. Krailsheime, (Penguin, 1966), 159.

26 Leo Tolstoy, *The Death of Ivan Ilyich,* trans. Lynn Solotaroff (Bantam Dell, 1981), 33.

27 Ibid.

28 Thomas Watson, "Time's Shortness," accessed 5 July, 2021, gracegems.org.

29 John Calvin, *The Institutes of Christian Religion,* vol. 1 Book 3 (The Westminster Press, 1960), 714.

is a detriment. Doctors have started to adjust practice by bringing families back to witness the CPR so that they can see everything was done to "save" their loved one. In a family meeting when a patient has died, doctors now use the word "death" instead of alternatives like "passed away," "departed," "asleep," "gone," and "slipped away" to eliminate confusion and confirm the finality. "Died" is one of the hardest words I have ever had to say to a family. In these moments, apathy is temporarily replaced by grief. But, like Ivan Ilyich, the last word uttered in death is "forget", and we are too weak to correct it.[30]

---

30 Leo Tolstoy, *The Death of Ivan Ilyich* trans. Lynn Solotaroff (Bantam Dell, 1981), 113.

Chapter 9
Application Questions

1. Memory is considered a function of the past. So how does memory relate to the future?

2. What are some ways society shows how much value is placed on future remembrance? Do you relate to the examples of the misplaced value in photography or childbearing? Do other examples come to mind?

3. What emotions rise up when you think about death? What is most unsettling about death to you?

4. How does future remembrance connect to actions like heroism, hedonism, and hoarding? Which do you struggle with the most?

5. Do you tend to be anxious or apathetic about death? Do you think about death often or rarely?

10

God's Redemption of Future Remembrance

A distorted viewpoint of future remembrance produces misguided purpose driven living. The self-centered orientation of the desire to be remembered needs to be unbent from an inward curvature to one that points back to God and His glory—the primary purpose of memory. In a distorted remembrance, fear springs from the necessity of others to remember you, but remembrance by others is flawed. Others fail through flawed memory, and others die themselves. Remembrance is existential to you, but the one remembering needs perfect memory and eternality.

Immutability and Eternality

God knows and sees all. He consults no one (Isa. 40:13–14). God's immutability guarantees the perfection of these attributes. "He has never changed and can never change in any smallest measure. To change would need to go from better to worse or worse to better. He cannot do either, for being perfect He cannot become more perfect, and if He were to become less perfect He would be less than God."[1] God's immutability dovetails with His eternality. To remain the same in past, present, and future implies that He will be so forever (Heb. 13:8). The psalmist connects immutability and eternality in Psalm 102, "Of old You founded the earth, and the heavens are the work of Your hands. Even they will perish, but You endure; and all of them will wear out like a garment; like clothing You will change them and they will be changed. But You are the same, and Your years will not come to an end." The earth is changing, but God will never change and will never end.

Eternality is fundamental to future remembrance. Man requires remembrance due to his earthly transience. "Before the mountains were born or You gave birth to the earth and the world, even from everlasting to everlasting, You are God" (Ps. 90:2). In contrast with God's eternality, the psalmist continues, "You turn man back into dust" (90:3a) and man "fades and withers away" (90:6). Due to death, another must exist that precedes birth and proceeds after death, and God's eternality encompasses the human's earthly lifespan. His remembrance never ceases. Memory demonstrates dependence of a transient being upon an eternal being who spans generation after generation. Creatures fight this notion of a dependence, but you can be comforted by God's remembrance of you.

So far, remembrance has only applied to the transient time on earth. However, God's eternal remembrance carries even greater significance in relationship to the eternality of the human soul. In death, the body is cast aside, but the soul lives. The remembrance of the soul and its well-being depend upon an eternal God. The psalmist reminds us, "Do not trust in princes, in mortal man, in whom there is no salvation. His spirit departs, he returns to the earth; in that very day his thoughts perish" (Ps. 146:3–4). The finite trusts the infinite who "will reign forever" (Ps. 146:10) and "who alone possesses immortality" (1 Tim. 6:16). Eternal remembrance is bound up in the mind of God.

---

1 A. W. Tozer, *The Pursuit of God*, Project Guttenberg ebook 2008, *39*.

Justice
··········

God's immutable eternality infuses through His other attributes with significant implications for the future. God's justice reigns from beginning to end. God's perfect future remembrance evokes terror for some and comfort for others. The fear rises from the reality that "there is no creature hidden from His sight, but all things are open and laid bare to the eyes of Him with whom we have to do" (Heb. 4:13). God knows each person; not one sin escapes notice. As Augustine confesses, "What is there in me that could be kept hidden from You, even if I refused to confess it to You? If I were to do that, I would only hide You from myself, not myself from You."[2] The future judgment by God accounts for every thought and deed. However, God's justice also brings comfort to the one who is treated unjustly. "For the LORD loves justice and does not forsake His godly ones; they are preserved forever, but the descendants of the wicked will be cut off" (Ps. 37:28). People do not want a just God to judge them, but they do want a just God to judge others on their behalf. However, all deserve the terror, and none deserves the comfort (Rom. 5:12). Future judgment awaits.

Lovingkindness
·····················

In harmonious tension with God's justice is His lovingkindness.... God's covenant-keeping love springs eternal. In the Bible, the comforting eternal nature of God's lovingkindness many times follows verses that address man's transience. King David follows the realities of man's days that are like the flower of the field that is blown away by the wind with the comforting contrast "But the lovingkindness of the LORD is from everlasting to everlasting on those who fear Him, and His righteousness to children's children" (Ps. 103:17). The frail, fading flower fears forgetfulness but we find permanence in the everlasting arms of the Father's lovingkindness. This connection of man's frailty to God's eternality through His lovingkindness serves a vital role in the redemption of remembrance. "To know that God knows everything about me

2 Augustine of Hippo, *Augustine's Confessions* (Sovereign Grace Publishers, 1971), 86.

and yet loves me is indeed my ultimate consolation."[3] But how is it possible for God to know everything about me and not exercise His justice?

REDEMPTION OF FUTURE REMEMBRANCE

The cross marks the intersection of justice and lovingkindness in judgment. The Son not only secured your present salvation at the cross but also your future salvation at the great white throne. Just as salvation is an act of God's remembrance, so will be His final salvation. God's grace through faith guarantees a position for sons and daughters in God's family, not only on earth but also in heaven, not only from wrath but also from the wrath to come.

When Christ died on the cross, His blood pardoned all those who believe, not just in the present but in the future. His blood "stains" much like the crimson worm found in Israel (Ps. 22:6). The female attaches herself to the tree. She lays her eggs under her crimson body. The eggs hatch and the larva feed on the mother's body. When the mother subsequently dies fixed to the tree, her body oozes crimson dye that stains the tree and also the larva for life.[4] After three days, the shell of the mom falls off the tree. The babies carry the crimson stains of the mother's death around the rest of their lives. For a Christian, the blood of Jesus stains permanently; sin is washed away for all eternity. Isaiah comments, "Though your sins are as scarlet, they will be white as snow" (Isa. 1:18a). The work of the cross is eternal.

The work of the cross contrasts to the laundry room in my childhood home. The laundry room was tucked away next to the kitchen. You would visit over and over again with dirty clothes, the same ones you washed the previous week. These clothes would be placed into the washing machine with the hope that all the stains would be removed. However, each load of laundry never came out perfectly clean, as stains remained. Worse than that, I remember mixing the white load with red socks, and the entire white load turned pink. Not so with Christ! All of your

3 R. C. Sproul, *The Intimate Marriage: A Practical Guide to Building a Great Marriage* (P&R Publishing 2003), 12.

4 "The Crimson or Scarlet Worm," 20 November, 2011, accessed 9 July, 2021. discovercreation.org

stains are removed through His blood. His red blood takes your dirty laundry and turns it white as snow, once and for all.

Christ is your hope not just in life but also in death. John recalled how Jesus reassured him when "He placed His right hand on me, saying, 'Do not be afraid; I am the first and the last, and the living One; and I was dead, and behold, I am alive forevermore, and I have the keys of death and of Hades'" (Rev. 1:17b–18). Christ conquered death in His resurrection, which guarantees your future resurrection. "For if we believe that Jesus died and rose again, even so God will bring with Him those who have fallen asleep in Jesus" (1 Thess. 4:14). Christ's death provides comfort in the face of death. Death is no longer the end but is now the means of passage from mortality to immortality.

Before he died on March 1, 1981, the last passage Martyn Lloyd-Jones, a Welsh medical doctor and preacher, read was "O death, where is your victory? O death, where is your sting? The sting of death is sin, and the power of sin is the law; but thanks be to God, who gives us the victory through our Lord Jesus Christ" (1 Cor. 15:55–57).[5] What a great passage to end your earthly race and start your heavenly one! Live with hope. Die with hope.

PROMISES OF FUTURE REMEMBRANCE

God's remembrance of His precious promises secures your future remembrance. The psalmist places his hope in God's future remembrance when he says, "He has remembered His covenant forever, the word which He commanded to a thousand generations" (Ps. 105:8). The covenants must be applied not just in the past and present but forever. His covenant-keeping love must endure forever. It cannot falter at any time. "'For the mountains may be removed and the hills may shake, but My lovingkindness will not be removed from you, and My covenant of peace will not be shaken,' says the LORD who has compassion on you" (Isa. 54:10–11). God's covenant remains though all else changes and fails. Here is the comfort for His people: "O afflicted one, storm-tossed, and not comforted, behold, I will set your stones in antimony, and your foundations I will lay in sapphires. Moreover, I

5 Jeremy Marshall, "Dr. Martyn Lloyd-Jones on Preparing for Death—by Rev. Iain Murray," accessed 9 July 2021, banneroftruth.org 17 July 2020.

will make your battlements of rubies, And your gates of crystal, And your entire wall of precious stones" (Isa. 54:11–13). The solace is permanence, an unshakeable foundation built upon the unshakeable covenant.

The promises of future remembrance find ultimate fulfillment in Christ. "For as many as are the promises of God, in Him they are yes" (1 Cor 1:20a). Jesus holds eternal souls in His eternal hands. "For this is the will of My Father, that everyone who beholds the Son and believes in Him will have eternal life, and I Myself will raise him up on the last day" (John 6:40). To face death is the last act of faith on earth. Do you trust in the eternal God's future remembrance? Future remembrance by others will fail, but future remembrance by Christ will prevail.

PERSONALIZATION OF FUTURE REMEMBRANCE

The promises of future remembrance apply not only to people generally but personally. Jesus addressed this personal knowledge to a crowd as He first warned of hypocrisy. Nothing is hidden from God's sight (Luke 12:2–3). Therefore, do not fear men who kill the body; but fear the One who has authority over your soul (see Luke 12:4–5). In this context, Christ then reminds the crowd of God's care. "Are not five sparrows sold for two cents? Yet not one of them is forgotten before God. Indeed, the very hairs of your head are all numbered. Do not fear; you are more valuable than many sparrows" (Luke 12:6–7). With God, all details are known. One adult averages around one hundred thousand scalp hairs and grows about twenty-five feet of hair in a lifetime.[6] Each hair on the head goes through a growth cycle that can last up to seven years. The number of hairs changes daily with growth and loss influenced by age. God knows the specific number for each person on the planet. God values you.

Christian, how do you know God values you? Because God paid the highest price, the precious blood of His Son to redeem you (1 Peter 1:18–19). "Child of God, you cost Christ too much

6 Bill Bryson, *The Body: A Guide for Occupants* (Penguin Random House, 2019), 19–20.

for Him to forget you."[7] God will not forget you now, and He will not forget you in the future.

Jesus, the Morning Star, knows all the stars by name (Ps. 147:4). Surely, the Good Shepherd knows all of His sheep by name (John 10:3). Yes, God knows your name on earth, and He will know your name in heaven. To the overcomer, God will give "a new name written on the stone which no one knows but he who receives it" (Rev 2:17b). This special name signifies your value. You walked the earth as a Jacob, Simon, or Saul but will walk in the new earth as an Israel, Peter, or Paul. When God gives a new name, He gives a new identity. God has inscribed you on the palm of His hands; He will not forget you (Isa. 49:15–16).

A name identifies not just on earth but also for eternity. In the book of remembrance, God records the names of those who esteem His name (Mal. 3:16). This book of names serves to distinguish the righteous from the wicked. Those recorded are God's own possession (Mal. 3:17). The names written in the book will be the names confessed by Christ before the Father (Rev. 3:5); these names are written in His blood (Rev. 13:8).

Is every person's name written in the Lamb's book of life? Is this book simply a record of every life lived on earth? The sobering answer is no. The wicked forsake God, and God forsakes them. The wicked deceive themselves to believe that God forgets. "He says to himself, 'God has forgotten; He has hidden His face; He will never see it'" (Ps. 10:11). But God sees and remembers all. The wicked "will give account to Him who is ready to judge the living and the dead" (1 Peter 4:5).

What is the judgment rendered by God for unrighteousness? Forgetfulness. "You have rebuked the nations, You have destroyed the wicked; You have blotted out their name forever and ever. The enemy has come to an end in perpetual ruins, and You have uprooted the cities; the very memory of them has perished, but the LORD abides forever" (Ps. 9:5–7). God blots out the wicked. The wicked stand at the throne, and God says, "I never knew you." The punishment is dire. "If anyone's name was not found written in the book of life, he was thrown into the lake of fire" (Rev. 20:15). How important is your name? It is a matter of eternal life and death.

7 Charles H. Spurgeon, "God's Memorial of His People" in The Complete Works of C. H. Spurgeon, vol. 61, Sermon No. 3441 (Delmarva Publications, 2015).

THE EFFECTS OF REDEMPTIVE REMEMBRANCE

On Saturday evenings, smoke filled the thick Texas air with the smell of barbecued hamburgers. The smell would settle in the porch of my childhood home: dinner was coming. The porch served as a place not just to smell burgers but as a place to gather and eat them. Porches are designed for lingering, and the longer you lingered the more you smelled like the smoke trapped under the overhang. Smoke seeps into your clothing and is absorbed into your skin. The truths of remembrance cling to you like smoke. The more time you spend in meditation on future remembrance, the more it permeates everyday life. When you leave the porch and walk through life, you still smell like its smoke. Redeemed future remembrance infuses into your walk in the forms of peace, perseverance, and purpose.

PEACE

Peace is the absence of worldly fear (John 14:27). It anchors the soul in a shaking world. Peace transcends tribulation (John 16:33). The transformation of future remembrance anchored in Christ's redemption brings peace (Rom. 5:1). He rendered "powerless him who had the power of death, that is, the devil, and might free those who through fear of death were subject to slavery all their lives" (Heb. 2:14b–15). This freedom from bondage supplies a peace that "surpasses all comprehension" (Phil. 4:8). It baffles a searching world that desperately desires peace but searches in all the wrong places. "You made us for yourself, and our hearts find no peace until they rest in you."[8] The restless find rest in Christ. Thomas Watson writes,

> We are in perpetual hurry, in a constant fluctuation; our life is like the tide; sometimes ebbing, sometimes flowing; here is no rest; and the reason is because we are out of center. Everything is in motion till it comes at the cen-

8 Augustine, *Confessions*, trans. R. S. Pine-Coffin, 1992, 21.

ter. Christ is the center of the soul; the needle of the compass trembles till it comes to the North Pole.[9]

Without a Christ-centered compass, the world wobbles and wanders. Rest is only found at the foot of the One who is unchanging. In Christ, you no longer need to strive for something else to satisfy; He is all you need.

No fear of death

The most famous psalm in the Bible says, "Even though I walk through the valley of the shadow of death, I fear no evil, for You are with me; Your rod and Your staff, they comfort me" (Ps. 23:4). Over many centuries, saints memorized and whispered these words to their own souls in times of affliction and in the presence of death. These verses remind the Christian of the comfort of God's presence in the looming shadows of death.

While writing this book, I witnessed a walk of peace in the face of death. My father-in-law, Lonnie Wick, was unexpectedly diagnosed with cancer. He quickly went from walking four miles on the beach to barely walking four steps in his house. After the diagnosis, he lived only eighteen more days. The peace of Christ shined bright in those last days. "Our infirmities become the black velvet on which the diamond of God's love glitters all the more brightly."[10] All throughout, Lonnie reiterated how he had indescribable peace; he was not scared. Before his body was laid to rest in the ground, his soul was already at rest. How? Every day, he had deposited God's Word in His mind. He had not ignored death but resolved to approach death, not alone but with His Savior by his side. When his last day on earth approached, it simply reflected every other day of his life. And his last day on earth was truly his best day. His last day was the closest on earth he came to reflecting the image of Christ. Now every day is his best day as he is with Christ.

9 Thomas Watson, "Psalm 138," in *The Treasury of David*, vol. 1 (Thomas Nelson Publishers, 1984), 206.

10 Charles H. Spurgeon, "A Wafer of Honey," 8 February, 1906, Web. 16 July, 2021, spurgeon.org.

May I speak each word as if my last word.
And walk each step as my final one.
If my life should end today,
Let this be my best day.[11]

No fear in death
••••••••••••••••••••••

God is not just present before death; He is with us after death. This truth rings out, "For he will never be shaken; the righteous will be remembered forever. He will not fear evil tidings; his heart is steadfast, trusting in the LORD" (Ps. 112:6–7). The Christian stands on solid ground as God's remembrance traverses the chasm of death. God's eternal remembrance of you guarantees the application of His everlasting grace upon you. The bridge is through Christ's blood because "my Redeemer lives" (Job 19:25). A living Redeemer actively dispenses life-giving grace. "Grace is not blasted by death—but transplanted into a better soil. Grace is not a lease which soon expires—but an inheritance entailed forever."[12] Here is the beauty of grace: grace does not just survive death; it but flourishes in death.

"For me to live is Christ and to die is gain" (Phil. 1:21). The apostle Paul viewed life and death from a redemptive perspective. Paul balanced two joys, the fruitful labor on earth with the expectations of heaven with Christ while most battle two miseries, the weariness of living and the fear of dying.[13] For the Christian, dying is not a negative fear but a positive joy. How is this possible? Because the funeral for the body is actually a marriage for the soul.[14] At death, the soul is immediately in the presence of the Lord (2 Cor. 5:8). At the day of your birth, you met your mother; but at the day of your death, you meet your Lord. "Depend upon it, your dying hour will be the best hour you have ever known!"[15]

11 *The Valley of Vision,* ed, Arthur Bennett, 13th ed. (Edinburgh: The Banner of Truth Trust, 2014), 221.

12 Thomas Watson, "Time's Shortness," accessed 21 April, 2021, gracegems.org.

13 Richard Baxter, *Dying Thoughts* (Edinburgh: The Banner of Truth Trust, 2009), 13.

14 Charles H. Spurgeon, "The Death of the Christian," 9 September, 1855, Web. 16 July, 2021, spurgeon.org.

15 Charles H. Spurgeon, "Christ with the Keys of Death and Hell," 3 October, 1869, Web. 16 July, 2021, spurgeon.org.

Death inspires fears of dark oblivion. The light dims, and the tunnel narrows. The Christian's hope resides in the knowledge that the light will actually grow brighter, and the tunnel will widen. Death is not dark loneliness; rather, "the Christian is not afraid of death because he has the assurance that he will not be left alone."[16] Death temporarily separates from the living on earth, but death eternally ushers the soul into God's presence. God redeems death into a means of joy, an entry into His presence. You are not alone in life, and you are not alone in death.

No fear of frailty

The transformation from fear to peace continues in future remembrance with contemplation of human frailty. Rather than try to ignore or refute frailty, David requests, "LORD, make me to know my end and what is the extent of my days; let me know how transient I am. Behold, You have made my days as handbreadths, and my lifetime as nothing in Your sight; surely every man at his best is a mere breath" (Ps. 39:4–5). In the midst of vanity and iniquity, the psalmist places his hope in God (Ps. 39:7). The psalmist does not run away from his transience but finds rest in it. "Feathers swim upon the water—but gold sinks into it. Light, feathery people float in vanity—but serious Christians sink deep into the thoughts of their death."[17] David sank into the brevity of his days and trusted God.

Brevity of life refines believers (Ps. 90:12). Knowing that life is short and that the death can come any time urges us to make the most of our time on earth (Eph. 5:16). Not only is life short but also the day of death is unknown. Even if we did know our lifespans, would we want to? God gave Hezekiah fifteen more years, but those fifteen years did not yield blessing: troubles abounded with the Babylonians. Uncertainty compels readiness.

Time is short, but the timing is right. God numbers your days (Job 14:5). "There are two mercies to a Christian. The first is that he will never die too soon; and the second, that he will never die

16 Jeremy Marshall, "Dr. Martyn Lloyd-Jones on Preparing for Death—by Rev. Iain Murray," accessed 9 July 2021, banneroftruth.org 17 July 2020.
17 Thomas Watson, "Time's Shortness," accessed 21 Apr. 2021, gracegems.org.

too late."[18] A human being is invincible for the extent of those determined days. "My times are in Your hand" (Ps. 31:15a).

> *Plagues and deaths around me fly*
> *Till He bids I cannot die;*
> *Not a single shaft can hit*
> *Till the God of love sees fit.*[19]

In this brief but perfect length of time on earth, Christians find solace in the mortality of sinful flesh. The hope for the future rests not just in immortality but sinless immortality. A never-ending earthly existence with the presence of sin strikes terror into any Christian. Richard Baxter summarizes: "Would I have God make sinful man immortal upon the earth? When we are sinless, we shall be immortal."[20] The frailty of a sin-filled body inspires hope in the eternality of a sinless soul.

Human brevity relieves us of the burdens we bear because of our enemies. Upon witnessing the prosperity of evildoers, believers are commanded to "not fret" and "be not envious toward wrongdoers. For they will wither quickly like the grass and fade like the green herb." They are exhorted to "trust in the LORD and do good" and to "dwell in the land and cultivate faithfulness" (Ps. 37:1–3). God outlasts the enemy.

In the end, death's reign is brief in light of eternity. It marches toward its own expiration date. Death dies! Christ defeated and transformed death through His death and resurrection. No longer is death a source of fear, but a gateway to eternal life. The frailty of man is redeemed: it becomes an opportunity to trust an eternal, good God.

---

18 Charles H. Spurgeon, "The Death of the Christian," 9 September, 1855, Web. 16 July 2021, spurgeon.org.

19 John Ryland, "Sovereign Ruler of the Skies," 1 August, 1777, Web. 16 July, 2021, kenpulsmusic.com.

20 Richard Baxter, *Dying Thoughts* (Edinburgh: The Banner of Truth Trust, 2009), 93.

192

No fear of insignificance
••••••••••••••••••••••••••••••••

The Christian fights the desire for godly faithfulness to bring earthly fame of men. It is good to remember that many of the most faithful and heroic acts remain unknown. Faithful service practiced in obscurity misses the attention of men but catches the eye of God. Obscurity does not endanger faithfulness but rather endorses it as the service is for God rather than for men. In the church, the man-pleaser lurks, seeking fame by way of lip service or public leadership. God declares this is not who is significant in His eyes. "But to this one I will look, to him who is humble and contrite of spirit and who trembles at my Word" (Isa. 66:2). The least visible to man might be the most visible to God. True heroism blossoms in the bedroom, where nobody is watching but God. Here is the true mettle of a man or woman: humble integrity.

To clarify, God may choose to make faithfulness known on the earth. The gospel of Matthew records a woman who poured an alabaster vial of perfume on the head of Christ (Matt. 26:7). The disciples viewed the faithful act as a waste, but Christ corrected their assessment. He honored her costly sacrifice with this promise: "Truly I say to you, wherever this gospel is preached in the whole world, what this woman has done will also be spoken in memory of her" (Matt. 26:13). Jesus provided a helpful distinction about notoriety. The woman acted out of love for Christ and not for earthly fame. Christ honored her with what she did not seek—remembrance on earth. Earthly legacy may result from godly living, but it should not motivate godly living.

For a Christian, significance does not rest on remembrance by people but remembrance by God. The redemptive plan through Christ was born out of His everlasting love. He directed His love toward you, the object of His delight. Herein lies your significance: you are a beloved child of God through His unearned grace. You are unforgotten by the Unforgetting One. Significance with God removes the burden to perform for attention's sake and instead realigns the desire to obey for love's sake. Notoriety on earth fights for earned fame, while notoriety in heaven embraces unearned favor. Death is no longer a threat to your fame but, instead, confirms your significance. Death will not separate you from the love of Christ (Rom. 8.38–39). Death will unite you with Christ! His perfect love casts out the fear of death (1 John 4:18).

Significance dwells in your identity in Christ. His power transforms weakness into strength for His glory. "For the word of the cross is foolishness to those who are perishing, but to us who are being saved it is the power of God" (1 Cor. 1:18). Because of Christ, His power is perfected in weakness so that "[he] who boasts, boasts in the Lord" (1 Cor. 1:31). You no longer seek for others to proclaim your name but for your life to proclaim Christ's name. The desire for your significance is transformed into a desire to share about Christ's significance. This passion for Christ's fame led to these words by Count Zinzendorf to Moravian missionaries, "You must be content to suffer, to die, and to be forgotten."[21] It is better to be forgotten on earth and remembered in heaven. John Calvin's grave was unmarked on earth, but his life was marked by these words in heaven, "Well done good and faithful servant" (Matt. 25:21). These are the only words that truly matter. It is not about you putting your stamp on the earth, but God putting His stamp on you.

Fear God

Peace is the absence of the worldly fear of death, but peace is also the presence of the righteous fear of God. The fear of God is quite different from the fear of death. The fear of death is servile, while the fear of God is filial. Death is a cruel master; God is a kind father. The fear of death is a terror, while "the fear of the LORD is [a] treasure" (Isa. 33:6). The fear of the Lord does not lead to oppression but rather "leads to life so that one may sleep satisfied, untouched by evil" (Prov. 19:23). Fear of God results from a right remembrance of who He is and what He has done. "Only fear the LORD and serve Him in truth with all your heart; for consider what great things He has done for you" (1 Sam. 12:24). You revere Him because you depend on Him for everything. Your redemption rests in Him. "There is forgiveness with You, that You may be feared" (Ps. 130:4). God, the Forgiver,

21 Janet Benge, *Count Zinzendorf: Firstfruit—Christian Heroes Then and Now* (YWAM Publishing, 2006).

holds you in His fatherly hand. Herein lies a paradox: to fear God is to flee to Him. Fright leads to flight, not away from God but to Him. He is a refuge.

God's ways are beyond comprehension, too perfect to be understood. God "is someone whom none greater can be conceived."[22] This inconceivable One conceived of you and cares about you. So, like Solomon, "The conclusion, when all has been heard, is: fear God and keep His commandments, because this applies to every person" (Eccl. 12:13).

PERSEVERANCE

A right future remembrance replaces worldly fear with courage in perseverance. Perseverance leans into eternity with eyes lifted up to the reward of an everlasting tomorrow.

Weakness of the flesh

Paradoxically, recognizing your weakness in the present strengthens you to persevere in the future. Richard Sibbes states, "Weakness, with acknowledgment of it, is the fittest seat and subject for God to perfect His strength in; for consciousness of our infirmities drives us out of ourselves to Him in whom our strength lies."[23] The call to the Christian to persevere is a call to get help. Perseverance is not driven by self and how hard you can run and how much you can do. You are not called to blow wind into the sails of your own boat. Perseverance is born out of reliance on Christ. Here is Christ's own invitation: "Come to Me, all who are weary and heavy-laden, and I will give you rest. Take My yoke upon you and learn from Me, for I am gentle and humble in heart, and you will find rest for your souls. For My yoke is easy and My burden is light" (Matt. 11:28–30). Self-reliance prohibits rest, but Christ assures it. "His yoke is an easy yoke, His burden but as the burden of wings to a bird which make her fly higher."[24] The acknowledg-

22 Anselm of Canterbury, *The Major Works,* eds. Brian Davies and G. R. Evans (Oxford University Press, 1998), 87.

23 Richard Sibbes, *The Bruised Reed* (Edinburgh: The Banner of Truth Trust 1998), 96.

24 Ibid., 121.

ment of weakness eases the yoke and propels perseverance.

Not only do you need to remember your own weakness, but God also remembers your weakness. God extends the invitation to lighten the burden because He knows you are weak. "Thus He remembered that they were but flesh, a wind that passes and does not return" (Ps. 78:39). Instead of repelling God, weakness attracts His help all the more. As the Great Physician, He pours out His power on the brokenhearted (Ps. 147:3). Christ invites the weary and downtrodden to come. He "refuses none for weakness of parts, that none should be discouraged, but accepts none for greatness, that none should be lifted up with that which is of little reckoning with God."[25] In this way, God redefines greatness by dependency. Heroism is humility in weakness.

Waiting on the Lord

Perseverance establishes itself in weakness and expresses itself in waiting. Waiting is the fertile ground for an active memory to persevere. The mind continues to move quickly while the surrounding sufferings squeeze in. Weakness and waiting are connected in Isaiah as God comforts His people. The unweary God "gives strength to the weary and to him who lacks might He increases power" (Isa. 40:29). God is equal to the task of the comfort He promises His people. "Though youths grow weary and tired, and vigorous young men stumble badly, yet those who wait for the LORD will gain new strength; they will mount up with wings like eagles, they will run and not get tired, they will walk and not become weary" (Isa. 40:30–31). God blows away the righteous like stubble but blows the wind that lifts up the weary on eagles' wings. The weary wait, and God delivers.

Waiting relies on a right alignment of future remembrance. Future remembrances takes hold of the promises of God and casts them toward the future. These promises need to be handled with accuracy. In waiting for God, especially in trials, it is easy to misapply the promises. You expect what He did not actually promise. For instance, God does not promise to keep your life clear of storms, but He does promise to hold you in the midst of

25 Ibid., 23.

the storm (Ps. 118:6). God does not promise a hedge around your stuff but around your soul (Ps. 34:7). The presence of suffering is not a breach of God's promise; it is actually a fulfillment of it. "In this world, you will have tribulation" (John 16:33a). The one who orients memory to the future takes hold of the next part of the verse, "Behold, I have overcome the world" (John 16:33b).

Promises may be incorrectly applied to the worry of future suffering. Anxiety looks to the future but keeps the gaze focused on the things of this earth. An earthly gaze mishandles the promises. God does not promise grace for prospective trials of the future, but grace for the actual trials of the present. In waiting, the challenge for an active memory is to accurately recall the promises for the present to be applied to the present.

Paul supplies many examples of how to align the promises with right future remembrance. In writing to Timothy, he says, "For this reason I also suffer these things, but I am not ashamed; for I know whom I have believed and I am convinced that He is able to guard what I have entrusted to Him until that day" (2 Tim. 1:12). Paul persevered under great persecution with the view of future fulfillment of the promises by Christ.

Many saints through history sign their names in the margins of Scriptures next to these promises. One example is the martyr, Thomas Bilney. He waited in prison to be burned at the stake in England for standing up for the truths of Scripture. His Bible remains preserved at a library in Cambridge with the promise from Isaiah marked in pen, "When you walk through fire, you will not be scorched, nor will flame burn you" (Isa. 43:2b).[26] If a Bible were compiled of all the signatures of the saints next to the promises applied in suffering, "the whole volume might be scored in the margin of mementos of Christian experience."[27] Bilney, amongst others, teaches an important principle—wait in weakness; but do not wait empty-handed. Fortify your memory with eternal promises (1 John 2:25).

---

26 Charles H. Spurgeon, *Feathers for Arrows: Illustrations for Preachers and Teachers* (London: Passmore and Alabaster, 1870), 4–5.

27 Ibid.

Weightiness of glory
••••••••••••••••••••••••••••

Perseverance presses into these promises. Paul encourages the Corinthian believers with another future-oriented promise to "not lose heart, but though our outer man is decaying, yet our inner man is being renewed day by day" (2 Cor. 4:16). He takes stock of the weakness of man and the decay of the body, but contrasts the decay to the progressive transformation of the inner soul. Paul continues, "For momentary, light affliction is producing for us an eternal weight of glory far beyond all comparison" (2 Cor. 4:17). Affliction of the outer man is temporary compared to the glory that awaits the inner man that is eternal. Transience is a source of hope to the Christian as suffering has an end point. The hope is not just that suffering will end but that glory awaits, which has no end. How can this be?

Misery is momentary, while mercy is eternal. Christ secured mercy for all eternity (2 Tim. 1:9). Eternal mercy from ages past extends into the eternal future with application to the present. There is a bottom in misery but not a top in mercy. The believer, then, sets temporary suffering on one side of the scales and places the eternal weight of glory on the other. The weight of glory far surpasses the affliction to such a level that it catapults the affliction right off into the far distance. Perseverance waits in weakness for the weight of glory.

PURPOSE

Transformed future remembrance revolves around heavenly-mindedness. Heavenly-mindedness restores vision, revealing what is otherwise invisible. The believer looks "not at the things which are seen, but at the things which are not seen; for the things which are seen are temporal, but the things which are not seen are eternal" (2 Cor. 4:18).

In many ways, heavenly vision is similar to night vision—and not unlike the loosejaw fish's sight in the dark depths of the ocean. The fish has a unique fluorescent protein to be able to see red, a color outside of the blue-green spectrum that other deep-sea creatures see.[28] The loosejaw projects two powerful beams of red light from under each eye that stay lit all the time without detection by other predators or prey to allow the fish to hunt fearlessly and effectively. Similarly, the Christian's heavenly "goggles" remove the fear of death and clarify the purpose of life. The Christian sees with a transformed vision through the redemptive red blood of Christ.

Heaven: the Prize

With transformed future remembrance, the glow of heaven is visible while the glitter of earth dims. The resilient jewels of heaven surpass the fading flowers of earth. The Christian deposits treasure in heaven's storehouses where "neither moth nor rust destroys, and where thieves do not break in or steal" (Matt. 6:20). The uncertainty of earthly riches is turned into "everlasting wealth. Whatever is given to Christ is immediately touched with immortality."[29] Hoarding in heaven is for the wise but not the spiritually weak because the greatest deposits happen in the hardest times. Blessed are the persecuted for their reward in heaven is great (Matt. 5:11–12). Heavenly "goggles" enabled the joyful seizure of property by the persecuted early church because they knew they had a "better possession and a lasting one" (Heb 10:34). Life is one long lesson in loosening your grip on this world to lay hold of the next. Luther states, "I have held many things in my hands, and I have lost them all; but whatever I have placed in God's, I still possess."[30] Here is the key to heavenly hoarding: entrust the treasure to the right Treasurer.

God is not just the holder of the treasure but the rewarder of the treasure (Heb. 11:6). The Rewarder must remember to reward, and He does. "For God is not unjust so as to forget your work and the love which you have shown toward His name, in having ministered and in still ministering to the saints" (Heb. 6:10). The good deeds done on earth empowered by the Spirit will

28 Jonathan Balcombe, *What a Fish Knows,* Scientific American (2017), 35.

29 A. W. Tozer, *Born After Midnight* (Moody Publishers, 2015), 107.

30 J.H. Merle D'Aubigné, *History of the Great Reformation of the Sixteenth Century in Germany, Switzerland, &c.,* trans. H. White, vol. 4 (Robert Carter, 1846), 183.

be remembered in heaven. As you work hard in your earthly job, you do it for the Lord rather than for men "knowing that from the Lord you will receive the reward of the inheritance. It is the Lord Christ whom you serve" (Col. 3:23–24). The remembrance by God to reward motivates you to run hard for the prize because "your toil is not in vain" (1 Cor. 15:58). Paul pressed hard toward "the goal for the prize of the upward call of God in Christ Jesus" (Phil. 3:14). The prize of divine glory far surpasses the vainglory of this earth.

Heaven: the Place

Heavenly goggles direct your eyes to the heavenly prize but also the heavenly place. Paul continues in 2 Corinthians, "For we know that if the earthly tent which is our house is torn down, we have a building from God, a house not made with hands, eternal in the heavens" (2 Cor. 5:1). The believer groans for an eternal home, a place of permanence. On earth, the longing is intensified by hints of heaven. These hints "are not the thing itself; they are only the scent of a flower we have not found, the echo of a tune we have not heard, news from a country we have never yet visited."[31] These hints point to something better yet to come. Do not be deceived into the belief that these hints are the evidence that is earth is the only and best thing. The hints are just crumbs of the feast to come, not meant to satisfy but to make you long for more. God only provides crumbs so that you do not mistake this earth for your final home.[32] "Christian optimism is based on the fact that we do not fit in the world."[33] It is a source of joy to know that this is not all there is. Something better exists. The heavenly-minded do not attempt to make earth into heaven. They instead enjoy the crumbs as crumbs, a foretaste of the divine banquet.

31 C. S. Lewis, "The Weight of Glory," 8 June, 1942, Web. 21 July, 2021, wheelersburg.net

32 C. S. Lewis, *The Problem of Pain* (HarperOne, 2001), 116.

33 G. K. Chesterton, *Orthodoxy* (Moody Publishers, 2009), 121.

Heaven: the Person

A heavenly-focused Christian is a pilgrim passing through on a journey "looking for the city which has foundations, whose architect and builder is God" (Heb. 11:10). This journey on earth with the gaze toward the celestial gates simply follows the pilgrimage of Jesus. Jesus, a sojourner on earth, comforted the disciples with these words: "In My Father's house are many rooms; if that were not so, I would have told you, because I am going there to prepare a place for you. And if I go and prepare a place for you, I am coming again and will take you to Myself, so that where I am, there you also will be" (John 14:2–3). Jesus comforted pilgrims with the promise of passage to a permanent place He will prepare. He fixed His gaze on the cross so that you can now fix your gaze on Him. He humbly walked through earth and now sits glorified at the right hand of the throne in heaven (Heb 12:2). His path is your path. His permanence is your permanence. His place is your place.

The hope of an eternally minded believer is that "our citizenship is in heaven" (Phil. 3:20a) but the eager expectation extends beyond the place and prize of heaven to the person in heaven. The longing for the place is based on the presence of Christ. "We are of good courage, I say, and prefer rather to be absent from the body and to be at home with the Lord" (2 Cor. 5:8). The Light of heaven is the source of endless delight. You will be united with Him and "be like Him, because we will see Him just as He is" (1 John 3:2). The longing to see Him in all His glory will be fulfilled in a glorious transformation. You will not just be with Him but be like Him.

Heaven: the Purpose

The heavenly "goggles" help keep your gaze on the person of Christ while you walk amongst the distractions of this earth. With this heavenly focus, the purpose of life crystalizes. Paul concludes, "Therefore, we also have as our ambition, whether at home or absent, to be pleasing to Him" (2 Cor. 5:9). The aim remains the same, whether on earth or in heaven, to please Him.

You were made for a high calling, an eternal ambition that does not change even in death. The purpose remains constant while the place changes. The purpose of present memory and future remembrance align, to bring God glory.

Summary

A heavenly mindset transforms the corruptions of present memory and future remembrance. Grumbling about an earthly condition turns into groaning toward a heavenly one. Nostalgia, a longing for the past, bends toward a longing for a heavenly future. The realities of divine forgiveness displace bitterness over past wrongs done to you. Regret, anguish over what might have been, reaches toward a heavenly expectation for what is to come. Shame and false guilt melt away in the beauty of divine love and marvelous grace set upon you. Heroism, hoarding, and hedonism dissolve in the dewdrops of heaven. Apathy gives way to expectancy, and anxiety finds solace in the surety of a heavenly future. The transformation of memory on earth requires an unbending of memory from its inward curve to self into an upward curve toward God. The unbending of your memory depends not on you or others but on God. His redemption transforms your memory.

Chapter 10
Application Questions

1. How do God's eternality and immutability link to each other? How does the cross bring together God's justice and lovingkindness?

2. Why are names significant to God? How do names play a role in future remembrance?

3. How can a Christian have peace? How would you explain the relationship between the fear of God and the fear of death?

4. How is waiting on the Lord active and not passive? How does your view of God influence your view of waiting?

5. Read 2 Corinthians 5:1–9. How do heavenly "goggles" affect present daily living?

11

God's Forever Remembrance

The transformation of memory starts on earth and comes to a full realization in heaven. "For now we see in a mirror dimly, but then face to face; now I know in part, but then I will know fully just as I also have been fully known" (1 Cor. 13:12). God will complete the transformation of memory (glorification). Corrupted memory will no longer function like a tormenting cudgel. Memory will stop revolving around self. Through the cross, the cudgel of memory will be transformed into a crown of glory. Memory in heaven will not beat you away from God but serve as a means to glorify and enjoy Him forever. The gravity pull toward self is transformed into an irresistible attraction to God.

Memory in the presence of God will not just be oriented toward God but be in Him. The divine transformation fulfills the prayer of Christ. "The glory which You have given Me I have given to them, that they may be one, just as We are one; I in them and You in Me, that they may be perfected in unity" (John 17:23–24). Grasping the profound implications of memory perfected through union in Christ is challenging, possibly tempting us to unbiblical speculation; nonetheless, reflecting on these implications is valuable. These reflections are by no means comprehensive, but they spur us to consider and meditate on heaven.

My childhood home had an attic like most houses do. The

pitch in the roof created a space for my family to store boxes, many of which were filled with memories forgotten for years until incidentally discovered upon the search for something else. I would climb up to look for Christmas lights only to discover my old blue baseball glove. What a joyful surprise! The glove would bring back happy memories of baseball in the summer.

Will heaven be like the attic with memories that are still accessible? Will accessible memories only be the joy-filled ones? What about those things that remind you of suffering and sin? What if a memory is attached to both joy and sorrow? Perhaps the same blue baseball glove that brings a smile also brings a frown as you recall the day you threw a baseball through the neighbor's window. Future memory in heaven is complex, but the purpose of memory remains the same, to bring glory to God and enjoy Him forever. So what will we remember and forget?

WHAT WILL YOU FORGET IN HEAVEN?

Forget the ark
....

Jeremiah provides one area of forgetfulness in heaven when he writes, "'It shall be in those days when you are multiplied and increased in the land,' declares the LORD, 'they will no longer say, 'The ark of the covenant of the LORD.' And it will not come to mind, nor will they remember it, nor will they miss it, nor will it be made again'" (Jer. 3:16). "Jerusalem will be by the throne of Jehovah" and there is no longer a need to remember the symbolic ark.[1] The presence of God in Jerusalem puts the people into a perpetual state of joy. Joy could not be further improved upon by remembrance of the ark because God's glory will overshadow the ark. It is hard to fully comprehend the transformation of memory in heaven in God's presence, but Jeremiah gives a glimpse.

---

1 Carl Friedrich Keil and Franz Delitzsch, "Commentary of Isaiah 65." Keil & Delitzsch Old Testament Commentary, https://www.studylight.org/commentaries/eng/kdo/isaiah-65.html. 1854–1889.

Forget the former trouble
••••••••••••••••••••••••••••••••

> In speaking of the new heavens and new earth, Isaiah states,
> Because he who is blessed in the earth will be blessed by the
> God of truth; and he who swears in the earth will swear by
> the God of truth; because the former troubles are forgotten,
> And because they are hidden from My sight! For behold, I
> create new heavens and a new earth; and the former things
> will not be remembered or come to mind. For be glad and
> rejoice forever in what I create.
> (Isa. 65:16–18a)

Former troubles will not be erased but rather not be dwelt
upon in any way that diminishes joy. The joy of redemption will
overwhelm the misery such that the misery will no longer be a
source of pain. Memory, then, is not punitive but pedagogical
(instructive) to pointing us to the greatness and glory of Christ.

It is too simple to classify memories as good and bad, but to
look at memory by its effect upon the worshipper. The worshipper
in heaven will forget anything that will diminish joy and worship
of God and will remember everything that enhances joy and
worship of God.[2] God will wipe away tears, but this does not
wipe away memory. The redemption story includes the scars.

This reminds me of one of the longest nights of my life in
residency. While working in the pediatric ICU, a teenage boy
arrived by ambulance in critical condition. He had recently been
diagnosed with a mediastinal mass. The mediastinum refers to a
space in the chest that contains important organs like your heart,
trachea, esophagus, and also smaller things like blood vessels
and lymph nodes. This athletic teenage soccer player now faced
death because one of the small things—his lymph nodes—had
grown large enough with lymphoma (a type of cancer) to push
on all the important organs and blood vessels. When I saw him,
his mouth was blue; and within ten minutes of arrival, his mouth
was breathing through a tube. Another tube was placed into his
left chest to drain fluid from his lung. Despite the best technology

2 John Piper, "What Will We Remember in Heaven?" 20 February, 2007, Web. 4
August, 2021, desiringgod.org.

and care, he almost died that night. If I rolled him onto his right side, his blood pressure would drop as the mass pressed on blood vessels. If I rolled him onto his left side, his oxygen level would fall due to the fluid in his left lung. That morning, emergency radiation treatment was started and shrunk the mass over the next few days. He survived. Later in the week, the tubes were removed and a port for chemotherapy was placed.

About a year later, I was on a pediatric anesthesia rotation at the same hospital. In walked the teenager, here for removal of the port. He was cancer free. We talked about the night he almost died, and the year-long treatment he had endured. His thankfulness grew as he recounted each phase of the journey from diagnosis to that night of near death, the radiation, the chemotherapy, and now the removal of the port. Thankfulness looked different each step of the way and overflowed now as he sat there healthy. He looked different now. His hair would grow back, but the scars remained from the chest tube and the port. The sites of the scars no longer elicited pain when touched. The sight of those scars reminded him of triumph.

In a much grander way, the story of redemption cultivates a growing thankfulness. Your thankfulness expands from salvation through sanctification on earth into glorification in heaven. Rather than remove the painful memories of the journey completely, perhaps these memories are transformed. Battles and heartache remain in the presence of the Savior, no longer causing pain but a sense of triumph. The *millstones* on earth become *milestones* in heaven.

WHAT WILL YOU REMEMBER IN HEAVEN?

What will you remember in heaven? Isaiah and Jeremiah looked at the new heavens and new earth, but John also looked on a heavenly scene in Revelation, the last book of the Bible.

Remember God as King

John, the author of Revelation, describes heaven filled with vivid colors of the throne surrounded by a rainbow (Rev. 4:3) and a sea of glass (Rev. 4:6). He walks through the door of heaven and witnesses worship. The worship of God never ceases (Rev. 4:8a). The unending worship implies something about God: He cannot be forgotten. The four living creatures say, "Holy, holy, holy is the Lord God, the Almighty, who was and who is and who is to come" (Rev. 4:8b). God is holy, sovereign, omnipotent, and eternal. His everlasting majesty draws forth eternal praise. The seraphim worship the King for His infinite greatness.

Remember God as Creator

The scene in heaven moves to the twenty-four elders who join in worship. These elders fall down before Him and cast their crowns before the throne (Rev. 4:10). The elders say, "Worthy are You, our Lord and our God, to receive glory and honor and power; for You created all things, and because of Your will they existed, and were created" (Rev. 4:11). Here, the elders emphasize the worship of God as Creator of all things. Creation bows at the feet of the Un-created One.

In the garden of Eden of Genesis, Adam's worship would have centered on God as King and Creator, but sin entered the garden. Sinful man was driven from the presence of a holy God. The next scene in Revelation builds upon the tension of this separation with the question, "Who is worthy to open the book and to break its seals?" (Rev. 5:2).

Remember Jesus as Redeemer

John weeps because no one is found worthy to open the book (Rev. 5:4). All fell short of God's matchless holiness. But one of the elders comforts John. "[T]he Lion ... of Judah, the Root of David, has overcome so as to open the book and its seven seals" (Rev 5:5). John looks for the Lion and sees the Lamb, standing as if slain (Rev. 5:6). The living creatures and elders direct worship to the Lamb of God with a new song, "Worthy are You to take the book and to break its seals; for You were slain, and purchased for God with Your blood men from every tribe and tongue and people and nation. You have made them to be a kingdom and priests to our God; and they will reign upon the earth" (Rev. 5:9–

10). Then myriads of angels join with the words "Worthy is the Lamb that was slain to receive power and riches and wisdom and might and honor and glory and blessing" (Rev. 5:12). The praises culminate with every created thing in heaven and earth saying, "To Him who sits on the throne, and to the Lamb, be blessing and honor and glory and dominion forever and ever" (Rev. 5:13).

The worship of the Lamb culminates with remembrance of redemption. The worshippers see the scars of the slain Lamb and remember that the Lamb shed His blood to purchase His own who will reign with Him. The scars of Christ will be an eternal reminder of God's grace. Thomas saw the resurrected Christ with holes in His hands and a wound in His side and proclaimed, "My Lord and my God" (John 21:28). All creation will see the slain Lamb and worship Him forever. Richard Baxter wrote, "Mercies remembered must be the matter of our everlasting thanks."[3] This refrain continues in the interlude between the opening of the sixth and seventh seal: "Salvation to our God who sits on the throne, and to the Lamb" (Rev. 7:10). The worshippers hold up palm branches in their hands and celebrate the Lamb who no longer sits on a donkey but on the throne.

Another scene in heaven takes place on the sea of glass. The victorious sing the song of Moses and the song of the Lamb saying, "Great and marvelous are Your works, O Lord God, the Almighty; Righteous and true are Your ways, King of the nations! Who will not fear, O Lord, and glorify Your name? For You alone are holy; for all the nations will come and worship before You, for Your righteous acts have been revealed" (Rev. 15:3–4). These saints remember the song of Moses, the first song in the Bible, that was sung to celebrate victory over Pharaoh's army at the edge of the Red Sea. Now singing on the sea of glass, the saints will fulfill the prophecy of the ancient Mosaic song when the Lamb "will bring them and plant them in the mountain of Your inheritance" (Ex. 15:17). Memory of the song of Moses with fulfillment of prophecy magnify the praise of the Lord.

---

3 Richard Baxter, *Dying Thoughts* (Edinburgh: The Banner of Truth Trust, 2009), 72.

Remember Jesus as Victor
....

John captures a climactic scene in heaven with four hallelujahs. The final thunderous shout says, "Hallelujah! For the Lord our God, the Almighty, reigns" (Rev. 19:6). The memory of the worshippers recounts the battle and revels in the victory. The story of redemption resounds in victory. Herein lies the great mystery of God.

The first Adam worshipped God for His greatness as King and Creator. Sin and death entered into the world. But God had a way through Christ to transform the broken into the best worshippers of Him. God in the garden is the same God. However, the worshipper no longer worships God as King and Creator but also as Redeemer and Victor. The creature now praises God not just as His Maker but also as His Savior. How is this possible? Memory. The heavenly worshipper under the New Covenant now brings man into the nearness of the Father through the blood of the Son. "Our original robes were rent asunder in Adam, but Jesus clothes us with divine righteousness, far exceeding in value even spotless robes of created innocence."[4] Redemption does not just restore to the original garden state but enhances to an eternal state of worship. Memory's created purpose, to bring glory to God, will find its ultimate satisfaction in heaven.

Memory in heaven will magnify the worship of God. God created man with a memory not only to glorify Him on earth but also in heaven. The first Adam, in the garden of Eden, glorified God as King and Creator but fell into sin. The second Adam, Jesus, walked from the garden of Gethsemane to conquer sin and death on the cross. Jesus, the Redeemer and Victor, will be remembered forever by the saints in praise at the throne of heaven. He is worthy of all your worship now and all your worship forever.

4 Charles H. Spurgeon, *Gleanings among the Sheaves* (New York: Fleming B. Revell, 1869), 189.

Chapter 11
Application Questions

1. What will you forget in heaven? What will you remember in heaven? How does this inform your worship today?

2. How is worship deeper with memory of God not just as King and Creator but also Redeemer and Victor?

3. How has your understanding of memory changed by reading this book?

4. What changes will you implement to orient your memory back to it designed purpose, to glorify God and enjoy Him forever?

About Shepherd Press Publications

They are gospel driven.
They are heart focused.
They are life changing.

Our Invitation to You

We passionately believe that what we are publishing can be of benefit to you, your family, your friends, and your work colleagues. So we are inviting you to join our online mailing list so that we may reach out to you with news about our latest and forthcoming publications, and with special offers.

Visit:

www.shepherdpress.com/newsletter

and provide your name and email address

COUNSEL
FOR THE
HEART

**A RESOURCE for WORD-BASED
TRANSFORMATION and
PRACTICAL DISCIPLESHIP**